_____

to

_____

from

"Give to the one who begs!
Do not refuse the one who
wants to borrow [this book]!"
Matthew 5:42

AWKWARD BIBLE

Awkward Moments (Not Found In Your Average) Children's Bible - Volume #3
Copyright ©2018 Awkward Bible
Text Copyright ©2018 Awkward Bible
Illustration Copyright ©2018 Awkward Bible

Awkward Moments (Not Found In Your Average) Children's Bible - Volume #3
©2014 Awkward Moments. All Rights Reserved. First Printing: 2018.
ISBN-13: 978-0996613910
ISBN-10: 0996613919
BISAC: Humor / Topic / Religion
See all of our books at: www.AwkwardMomentsBible.com
Requests for any additional information should be addressed to info@awkwardmomentsbible.com

Written By: Horus Gilgamesh, horus@awkwardmomentsbible.com
Illustrated By: Agnes Tickheathen, agnes@awkwardmomentsbible.com

Media Inquiries: info@awkwardmomentsbible.com

Awkward Moments

Not Found In Your Average

Children's Bible

Volume #3

Written by **Horus Gilgamesh**
Illustrated by **Agnes Tickheathen**

"I feel like I 'saved' my family..."

I've found that one of the best ways to challenge somebody's deepest held beliefs is through something seemingly small, inconsequential, or even random. *Enter doubt* - something that shakes their idea of "truth" and opens the door just a crack, enough to let in new information and ideas, causing them to investigate a different perspective for the first time.

For me, this first bit of doubt came as a Christian parent, struggling with how best to discipline my children. So many pastors preach on the Biblical justification to use physical punishment when disciplining children, but over time I felt it was *wrong* to spank them. Then the door opened just a crack. One night, after watching the movie *Buck*, about a horse trainer who uses empathy and communication instead of punishment with horses, I realized that I wanted to guide my children gently, with love and trust, rather than spanking. If I'd never strike a defenseless animal, why would I strike my own children? However, it wasn't long before my personal epiphany came into direct conflict with respected Christian leaders like Dr. James Dobson who all seem very eager to reminder followers that the Bible clearly says things like:

"Do not withhold discipline from a child; if you strike him with a rod, he will not die." - Proverbs 23:13

I found myself constantly thinking - just because the Bible says something, does that make it… right? Does that make it… true? So, I began searching online, trying to reconcile what I'd been taught for so many years in church with what I *knew* in my heart to be true. In this particular case, I found that while the Bible doesn't discuss spanking specifically, there were countless articles from pastors using plenty of Bible verses just like this as "proof" of God's "plan" for effective parenting. Then I found an article from some guy named Horus, a retired ministry leader who used a startling illustration of this scripture to illuminate the horrific child abuse and even deaths stemming from this Biblical teaching that inspired the bestselling book on Christian parenting, *To Train Up A Child*. As I read accounts of parents using these Bible verses to justify the abuse of their own children, my heart broke - for my kids, for my faith, and for my fellow parents. *"What have we been doing to entire generations of kids?"* I wondered. I could feel Horus' angry tears in his writing and I joined him for a good cry, the first of many in my long journey of recovery from religion.

Seeing these two very different takes on just one Bible verse made me wonder - what else had I been believing that might not have been right or true? *Enter more doubt.* I began questioning everything I had gained over the last 13 years of faith, reading everything I could find to help me make sense of an emerging reality. It was then that I cautiously opened the door into Horus Gilgamesh's crazy world - illustrating even the most cherished of Bible stories in a way that forces readers to actually think for themselves. As he discussed parts of the Bible that I'd always taken for granted, so many "truths" I'd held dear suddenly seemed obviously, embarrassingly bizarre. Not just in my own life, but also how they are used to control entire cultures, including our own.

Horus' unique perspective from a life of ministry really helped me see both sides of various issues, from the compulsory love of a god I'd been taught to fear, to the similar oppression of diminishing myself to accept my role as a "depraved wretch" in order to receive His love in return. These are startling realizations and

Horus spoke right to my inner thoughts, fears and doubts like only a person also recovering from religion really could. This was all very reassuring at a very vulnerable moment in my life, and helped me see that I wasn't alone - this stranger was struggling too.

You see, once you realize you no longer believe in religion, your life immediately feels unbearably hard and lonely. Your identity is gone, along with a large part of your social circle. You feel confused and know you must eventually face this journey head-on. Not exactly easy if you're single, but combined with a Christian family and a life centered around church - it's terrifying! And, that's part of the problem with religion - you shouldn't be afraid of the repercussions of simply admitting to others, "I *don't* believe."

Reading Horus' books and articles encouraged me to keep searching for the truth, especially when I would encounter questions from believers. I know that at times I hurt people's feelings, though I know they simply wanted to save me from going to hell - a hell I no longer believe in. Some awkward moments, indeed

I worked on updating myself for about 2 years, keeping the things I was learning and experiencing to myself. My relationship with my husband and our children got better quickly. He saw it and wondered why, leading to a good, long talk about about it all. In a way I feel like I "saved" my family. This will always be my greatest accomplishments and I really don't know if I could have done it without Horus' help.

To think - a fake children's book changing people's lives! Getting to know Horus a little bit, I now know was no accident - he knows exactly what he's doing. The simplicity of illustrating scripture in the Awkward Moments Children's Bible books is pure genius. Seeing scripture after scripture in a satirically shocking form, it's impossible not to recognize just how gruesome, immoral, and downright silly so many of the Bible's teachings really are. Horus' work helped unlock the absurdity of my own beliefs and helped me process the doubts I was having. I understand so much more about the Bible now, making it much easier to stand by my rejection of it as a guide for daily life!

So, please - dig into this book with an open mind and a little willingness to admit that maybe not all "truths" are created equal - especially your own. Most of all - be honest as you read and don't be afraid to laugh out loud, if even at yourself!

A big thanks to Horus for keeping it real and adding humor to it all! The next round is on me.

Holly Akers
Orlando, FL

Chicken Or Egg?

In the beginning...

- Genesis 1:1

The Rainbow Covenant

Upon exiting the ark, Noah built an altar to the Lord and sacrificed some of each clean animal as burnt offerings to Him. The Lord was pleased with the aroma and thought, *"Never again will I curse the ground because of humans, even though everything about their hearts is evil since childhood."* He told Noah, *"The fear and dread of you will fall on every creature of the earth; into your hands I deliver them all."*

- Genesis 8:16 - 9:13

Inevitable, <u>Eventual</u> Death

When Methuselah was one hundred and eighty-seven years old, he begat Lamech. Then he lived another seven hundred eighty-two years and begat other sons and daughters. And all the days of Methuselah were nine hundred and sixty-nine years: and then he (finally) died.

- Genesis 5:25-27

The First Blood Covenant

When Abram was 99 years old, the Lord appeared and said, *"If you are perfect, I will make a covenant with you and make you <u>Abraham</u> - father of all nations! I will give you the land of Canaan for your many descendants, forever - as long as they keep <u>one</u> simple covenant. All you have to do is use a knife to mutilate your genitals by cutting a ring of flesh from the tip of your penis.*

Then you must mutilate the genitals of every child and purchased slave in your house. From now on, all of your descendants must also mutilate the genitals of every newborn baby boy when they are eight days old. All male genitals must be mutilated to bear the mark of my covenant. Any man whose genitals are not mutilated will be 'cut off' from the family! This agreement will continue <u>forever!</u>"

Abraham agreed with the Lord's covenant and mutilated his own genitals before mutilating the genitals of his sons and slaves.

- Genesis 17
(summarized)

[About 6,000 years *before* Louis Pasteur discovered the germ.]

(Another) Blood Covenant

Moses came down the mountain and told the people of the Lord's instructions and regulations. They all responded as one, *"We will do everything the Lord has commanded."*

Moses carefully wrote down all of the Lord's instructions and got up the next morning to build an altar and twelve pillars. He sent some of the young Israelite men to present burnt offerings and sacrifice bulls as peace offerings to the Lord.

Moses drained half the blood from these animals into bowls and splattered the rest of the blood against the altar. Then he read the Book of the Covenant aloud to the people who again responded as one, *"We will do everything the Lord has commanded. We will obey."*

Moses splattered the remaining blood all over them, saying, *"This is the blood of the covenant the Lord has made with you."* [Then a bunch of them went up the mountain for snacktime with the Lord.]

- Exodus 24:3-12

There Will Be (Even More) Blood

After Moses had been gone for 40 days, the people were unsure what had become of him and asked Aaron, *"Make us some gods that will lead us."* So, Aaron took all of their gold jewelry and melted it down to make a golden calf which they celebrated as their Lord.

Up on the mountain, this made the Lord furious, saying, *"Leave me alone so my fierce anger can blaze against them and destroy them all!"*

Moses told the almighty Lord to calm down and the Lord did as He was told, changing His mind about the evil He threatened to bring on His people. But, when Moses saw the celebration and the golden calf he smashed the Lord's stone tablets to pieces at his feet and ground the golden calf into powder which he made his people swallow.

Moses commanded, *"Whoever is for the Lord, take your swords and kill everyone else - even your brothers, friends, and neighbors."* So, they killed 3,000 of their friends and family and were blessed for their service to the Lord. Later on, the Lord smote the remaining survivors.*

- Exodus 32, summarized

*Except, of course, Aaron and his brother Moses who were both blessed.

Th T n ᴄᴏmmɑn m nts™

Then the Lord told Moses, *"Bring me two **new tablets** and I will write the **same words** that I wrote on the original tablets which you destroyed."* Moses stayed on the mountain for forty days and forty nights with the Lord without eating any bread or drinking any water and the Lord re-wrote the terms of His covenant, **The Ten Commandments™**, on the stone tablets. When Moses brought them down the mountain to share with the people, his face was radiant!

- Exodus 34 summarized

The Right To Discriminate

God told Moses, *"In all future generations, if any of Aaron's descendants have **any** physical defect, he may **never** approach the altar to present special gifts to the Lord. Not if he is: blind, lame, disfigured, or deformed. Not if he has a broken foot, arm, is dwarfed, or has a hunched back. Not if he has a defective eye, or skin sores, or scabs, or has damaged testicles. Yes, he may eat from the food offered to God, but may **never** approach the altar or enter the room behind the inner curtain, for this would **defile** my holy places. I am the Lord who makes them holy."*

- Leviticus 21:16-23

Sticks And Stones

In the wilderness, a man was discovered picking up a stick on the Sabbath day. He was taken before the assembly and the Lord told Moses, *"This man must be put to death! Everyone must take him outside the camp and stone him!"* So, they did.

- Numbers 15:32-26

Fighting God's Battles

Suppose someone secretly entices you - even your own brother, your son or daughter, your beloved wife, or even your closest friend - and says, *"Let us go worship other gods."* They might suggest that you worship the gods of those who live nearby or come from the ends of the earth.

Do not give in or listen! Have no pity, and don't spare or protect them. **You must put them to death!** Strike the first blow yourself, and the others must join in.

- Deuteronomy 13:6-9

Off With Her Hand!

If two men are fighting and a wife tries to rescue her husband from being killed and touches the private parts of the other man, you shall cut off her hand. Do **not** show her **any** pity!

— Deuteronomy 25:11-12

Family Issues

In exchange for God's help killing the Ammonites, Jepthah vowed to kill whoever came out of his home first as a burnt offering. Upon returning, his **only** daughter came out, dancing and playing her tambourine! He yelled, *"You've devastated me and brought me misery! I made a vow to God that I can't break!"*

She said, *"You've given your word to God and must do to me as you promised. Give me two months to cry with my friends because I will die a virgin."* Two months later Jepthah did to her as he vowed. She was a virgin. Thus, **the** custom.*

- Judges 11:30-39

*Uh... what custom?

The Golden Hemorrhoids
(And Killer Mice)

The Philistines captured the Ark of the Covenant.
So, the Lord sent a fury of plagues by His heavy hand -
hemorrhoids and mice to torture and kill all the Philistines in towns
where the Ark traveled. The Philistine priests thought that if they
sent the Ark back to Israel with a guilt offering and the plagues
stopped, they would know it was God who was punishing them.
So, they molded five hemorrhoids and five mice out of gold and put
them on a cart attached to two cows. Once the cows arrived in
Beth-shemesh, the people were overjoyed. They broke up the wood
of the cart and killed the cows as a burnt offering to the Lord.
Then the Lord killed 70 more men - just for looking in the Ark.

- I Samuel 4-6
summarized

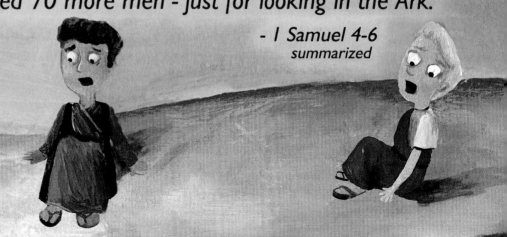

y Cherub And

After David's army killed everyone, he sang:

*"In **my** distress I cried out and the Lord heard **me**.
The earth quaked and trembled because of His anger.
Riding on a cherub, the Lord came down from heaven
with smoke pouring from His nostrils and fire leaping from
His mouth. The Lord's voice thundered as He shot arrows
and lightning to scatter and confuse His enemies.
The Lord rescued **me** from **my** powerful enemies
who hated **me**. He rescued **me** because
He is delighted in **me**. The Lord rewarded **me** for **my**
righteousness and He repaid **me** for **my** innocence."*

- 2 Samuel 21:22, 22:7-21
(summarized)

Convenient Condescension

Only **fools** say,
"There is no God."
They are **corrupt**.
Their actions are **evil**.
There is not one of them
who does **anything** good.
Not one.

- Psalm 14:1

It's ttin ot In r

"So, take off all your clothes (and sandals)," God told Isaiah. Isaiah did as he was told and walked around naked and barefoot for three years. The Lord later warned others, "My servant has been walking around naked and barefoot for the last three years, a symbol of the terrible troubles I will bring upon Egypt!"

- Isaiah 20:2-3

The Creator Of All

*"I form the light **and** the darkness.*
*I make peace **and** create evil.*
*I, the Lord do **all** these things."*
                                    - God

                    - Isaiah 45:7

Jesus Said...

- Matthew 12:39-40
- Jonah 1:15-2:20

IN MEMORY

Stanley Almodovar III, 23

Amanda Alvear, 25

Oscar A Aracena-Montero, 26

Rodolfo Ayala-Ayala, 33

Antonio Davon Brown, 29

Darryl Roman Burt II, 29

Angel L. Candelario-Padro, 28

Juan Chevez-Martinez, 25

Luis Daniel Conde, 39

Cory James Connell, 21

Tevin Eugene Crosby, 25

Deonka Deidra Drayton, 32

Simon Adrian Carrillo Fernandez, 31

Leroy Valentin Fernandez, 25

Mercedez Marisol Flores, 26

Peter O. Gonzalez-Cruz, 22

Juan Ramon Guerrero, 22

Paul Terrell Henry, 41

Frank Hernandez, 27

Miguel Angel Honorato, 30

Javier Jorge-Reyes, 40

Jason Benjamin Josaphat, 19

Eddie Jamoldroy Justice, 30

Anthony Luis Laureanodisla, 25

Christopher Andrew Leinonen, 32

Alejandro Barrios Martinez, 21

Brenda Lee Marquez McCool, 49

Gilberto Ramon Silva Menendez, 25

Kimberly Morris, 37

Akyra Monet Murray, 18

Luis Omar Ocasio-Capo, 20

Geraldo A. Ortiz-Jimenez, 25

Eric Ivan Ortiz-Rivera, 36

Joel Rayon Paniagua, 32

Jean Carlos Mendez Perez, 35

Enrique L. Rios, Jr., 25

Jean C. Nives Rodriguez, 27

Xavier Emmanuel Serrano Rosado, 35

Christopher Joseph Sanfeliz, 24

Yilmary Rodriguez Solivan, 24

Edward Sotomayor Jr., 34

Shane Evan Tomlinson, 33

Martin Benitez Torres, 33

Jonathan Antonio Camuy Vega, 24

Juan P. Rivera Velazquez, 37

Luis S. Vielma, 22

Franky Jimmy Dejesus Velazquez, 50

Luis Daniel Wilson-Leon, 37

Jerald Arthur Wright, 31

A Recipe for Disaster

If a man has sex with a man as one does with a woman, both have committed an abomination and shall surely be **put to death**; their blood is on their own heads.

- Leviticus 20:13

God's wrath is revealed against wicked sinners who give into shameful lusts of sexual impurity as they degrade their bodies with one another. Both the women and the men exchange natural sexual relations for unnatural ones. Men commit shameful acts with other men and receive the due penalty for their error. They know that by God's righteous decree, **they must die** for their actions.

- Romans 1:18-32

Happy New Year!

Eight days later, when the baby's genitals were mutilated *[per The Law]*, He was named Jesus, the name given by the angel before He was conceived.

- Luke 2:21

[4,000 years after Abraham, still 1,800 years before Pasteur.]

Like Father, Like Son

"Whoever denies me before men on earth, I will deny before my Father in heaven. Do not think I have come to bring peace on earth. **I do not bring peace, but a sword!**" - Jesus

- Matthew 10:33-34

"But now, take your money and bags. If you don't have a sword, sell your cloak and buy a sword!" - Jesus

- Luke 22:36

Moments Later: Jesus prayed in agony as His sweat fell like great drops of blood to the ground.

- Luke 22:44

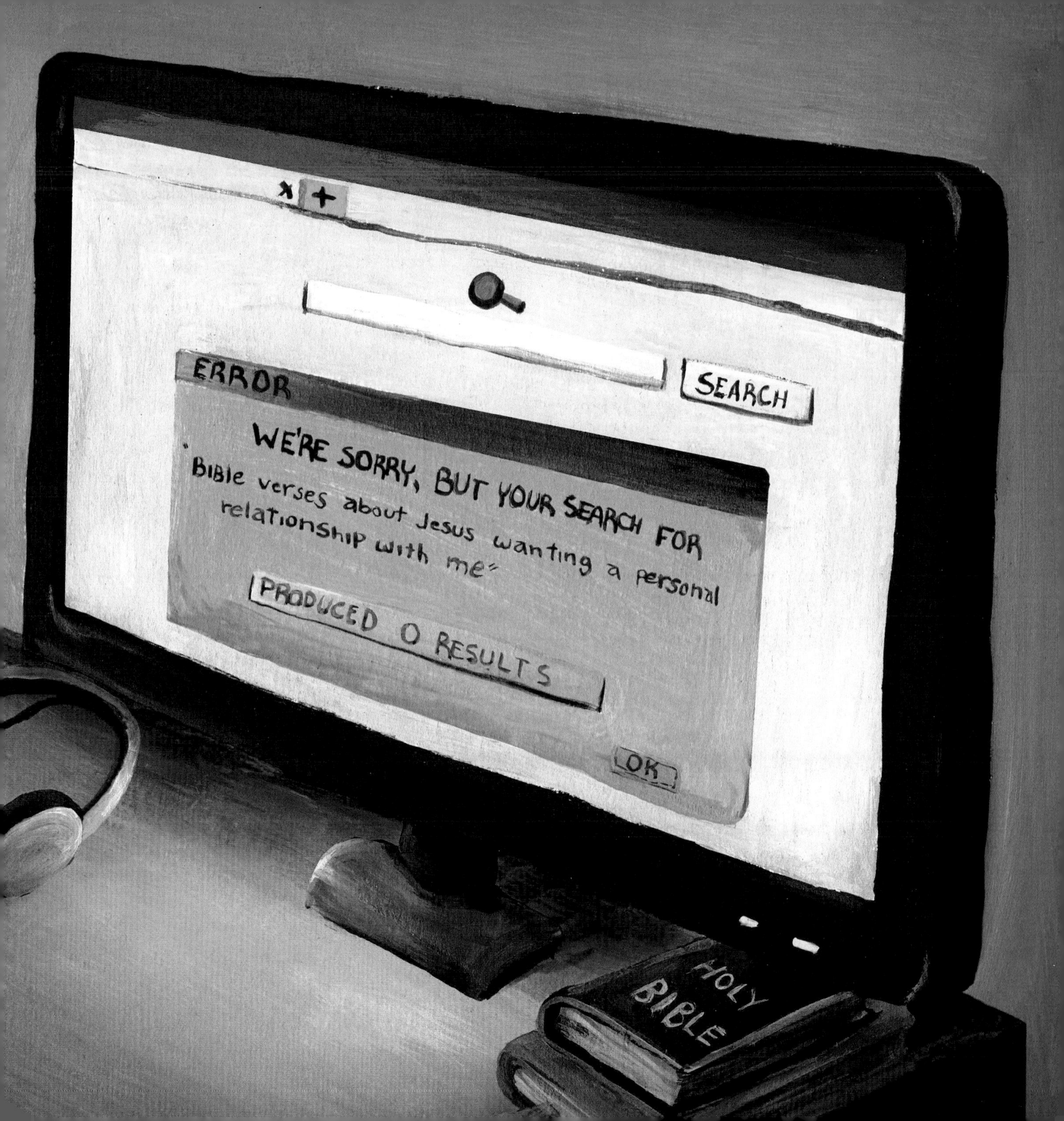
ERROR
SEARCH
WE'RE SORRY, BUT YOUR SEARCH FOR
"Bible verses about Jesus wanting a personal relationship with me"
PRODUCED 0 RESULTS
OK
HOLY BIBLE

A Whole New (Under)World

"God so loved the world, He gave His one and only Son, so that anyone who believes in Him will not perish but have eternal life. God didn't send his Son to judge the world, but that it might be saved through Him. Those who believe in Him will escape judgment, but anyone who does not believe in Him has already been condemned for not believing in God's one and only Son."

- John 3:16-18

"Anyone whose name was not found written in the Book of Life was thrown into the lake of fire... where the maggots that eat them will never die and the flames are never quenched!" - The Son

- Revelation 20:15, Mark 9:48

H#LY SP#R#T!

"Every sin can be forgiven **except** blasphemy against the Holy Spirit, which will **never** be forgiven. Speak against the Son of Man and you can be forgiven, but anyone who speaks against the Holy Spirit will **never** be forgiven, either in this age or in the age to come!" - Jesus

- Matthew 12:31-32

1 + 1 + 1 = Monotheistic Math

"For there are three that bear record in heaven, the Father, the Word, and the Holy Ghost: and **these three are one**. And there are three that bear witness in earth, the Spirit, the water, and the blood: **these three agree in one**." - Desiderius Erasmus, 1522

- I John 5:7–8

Jesus told the leper, *"Take all of the sacrificial offerings **as required by the law of Moses** to a priest so you can be purified."*

One bird must be slaughtered so the priest can dip a live bird, a stick, red yarn, and a branch into its blood and sprinkle it on you. Then you must shave off **<u>all</u>** your hair and bathe - staying outside for seven days. On the eighth day, bring three lambs, grain, and olive oil.* The priest will slaughter each animal as offerings and rub their blood and the oil on your right ear, thumb, and big toe.

This will make you purified before the Lord and the **offerings will belong to the priest.**

- Mark 1:44
- Leviticus 14:1-32

Budget options available.

FLOUR

OIL

In'-u M N-w.

Some people brought a blind man to Jesus, begging Him to heal the blindness. Jesus led the blind man by the hand outside the village and spit on his eyes, asking, *"Do you see anything?"*

The man looked around and said, *"I can see the people, but they look like trees."* Then Jesus laid his hands on the man's eyes. When he opened his eyes, the [unnamed and anonymous] man saw everything clearly [and promptly went into hiding].

- *Mark 8:22-25*

Of Dogs & Demons

A Canaanite woman came to Jesus and cried, *"Have mercy on me, O Lord, my daughter is possessed by a demon and suffering miserably."* Jesus did not reply, not saying a word. His disciples urged Him, *"Tell her to go away, she is bothering us."* He told her, *"I was sent <u>only</u> to the lost sheep of the house of Israel."* So, she knelt before Him and cried again, "Lord, help me." He replied, *"It is not right to take the children's bread and throw it to the **dogs**."* She agreed, *"Yes, Lord, but even the dogs eat the crumbs that fall from their master's table."* He told her, *"You have great faith, woman, and your wish is granted."*

Her [anonymous] daughter was healed instantly.

- Matthew 15:21-28

Live By Faith, Die By Faith

"If anyone is sick, call the leaders of the church and let them pray over him and anoint him with oil in the name of the Lord. Prayer offered in faith will heal the sick. The Lord will cure the sick. And if they have committed any sins, they will be forgiven."

Jesus said, "Your faith has cured you! Go in peace! Be cured!"

- James 5:14-15, Mark 5:34

An th r h nge ul

Jesus said, "I am the way and the truth and the life. No one can come to the Father except through me... If I had not come and spoken to them, they would not be guilty of sin; but now they have no excuse for their sin." There is no salvation in anyone else! There is no other name by which we can be saved. Nobody has any excuse for not believing in Him.

- John 14:6, John 15:22, Acts 4:12, Romans 1:20

A Time For Family

"Do you think I have come to bring peace to the earth? No, I have come to divide people against each other in their own house, three against two and two against three. Divided - son against father, mother against daughter, daughter-in-law against mother-in-law... A man's enemies will be those of his own household." - Jesus

- Luke 12:51-52
- Matthew 10:36

Th "[family] [Plus]" [unit]

Jesus' mother and brothers went to visit Jesus but couldn't get near Him because of a crowd. Someone told Jesus, *"Your mother and your brothers are outside and want to see you."* Jesus answered, *"Who is My mother and who are My brothers?"* Pointing to His disciples, He told them, *"My mother, brothers, and sisters are those who hear the will of the Lord and obey it!"*

- Luke 8:19-21

Director's Cut: Alternate Ending*

Jesus rose early on the first day of the week and drove seven demons out of Mary Magdalene. She went and told those who were mourning that Jesus was alive. They did not believe her.

Out in the country, Jesus appeared in a different form to two others who reported it to the rest; but they did not believe them either. Later Jesus appeared to the remaining disciples as they were eating and rebuked them for their refusal to believe those who had seen Him.

He told them, *"Go out and preach the Gospel to the world. He who believes and is baptized will be saved, he who doesn't believe will be condemned. These signs will accompany those who have believed: In my name they will drive out demons; they will speak in new tongues; they will pick up snakes with their hands; and when they drink deadly poison, it will not hurt them at all; they will place their hands on sick people, and they will get well."*

After Jesus had spoken, He ascended up into heaven where He sat the right hand of God. As instructed, the disciples went out and preached everywhere, and the Lord worked with them and confirmed His word by the signs that accompanied it [that is, until the invention of recording devices].

* Mark 16:9-20

Proud To Be A Fool

The message of the cross is foolishness to those who are doomed to perish, but it is God's power to those of us who are being saved. As the Scriptures say,

"I will destroy the wisdom of the wise and thwart the intelligence of the intelligent."

Where are the wise philosophers, scholars, and debaters of the world? God has turned the *wisdom* of this world into *foolishness*.

Since God in *His* wisdom made it so the world would never know Him through *their* own wisdom, He has used **our foolish preaching** to save those who believe in it.

- 1 Corinthians 1:18-21

Ee   Ff   G g

I will be a FOOL FOR JESUS

I will be a fool for Jesus

I will be a fool for Jesus

I will be a fool for Jesus

I will be a fool Jesus

— 1 Cor 4:10

In The Beginning...

"For the last time, it would be a proto-chicken, dammit," one old friend shouted at another just as his enormous fists exceeded the structural integrity of our bistro table, sending all of our cocktails, dinner plates, and silverware crashing loudly to the concrete floor. Judging by the looks we received from both patrons and staff, this was clearly not the sort of establishment accustomed to such spectacles of impassioned debate. Given the right mix of friends, I've yet to find a subject more entertaining than the great paradox - Which came first - the chicken or the egg?

At first blush the chicken-or-egg question might appear frivolous, nothing more than a silly riddle to tease the minds of children. But for me, the first three words of the Bible eventually led to a similar question; not concerning the origins of poultry, but of man, the universe, and perhaps most importantly for the context of this book - the genesis of gods and monsters. *"In the beginning…"* Which came first, god or man?

Before such a question can even be discussed, I must bring to light the existence of an ideology so prevalent that it comes with its own fancy eight syllable label: *pre-sup-po-sit-ion-al-is-m*. That is, for believers of many faiths, all of the questions worth asking have already been answered long ago by the sacred texts of their particular religious heritage. To many, there is absolutely no debate that god, their *particular* god, exists. As such, everything related to their god is obviously true, end of story. Or, as is commonly paraphrased in the most simplistic terms by some Christians, "The Bible says it, I believe it, and that settles it!" No questions necessary, or, in certain fundamentalist sects, allowed. After all, empirical knowledge must take a back seat to religious wisdom as we will see later on as we take a closer look at the Good Book.

One of the commonly used "gotcha" arguments you may have heard coming from those who look upon observational science with hostile denial goes something along the lines of, "But, something can't come from nothing! Therefore, someone obviously *had* to create it all in the first place!" Almost too conveniently, this bias helps them presuppose that this 'someone' just happens to be the *same* god of

their own familial, geographic, and/or cultural persuasions (while, of course, ignoring, discounting, or even going to war with those of dissimilar faiths). What are the odds, right? They are so blessed that their God just happens to be the only true God who just happened to have created the entire universe with them right in the center. Lucky!

Something can't come from nothing? For a moment let's disregard how modern cosmology, particle physics, and quantum mechanics all suggest the inverse is true. Instead, let's ask the simple followup question, "Well, then, who or what created your particular God to begin with?" While the commonly convenient response may conclude that their god defies any natural criteria by being infinite in time and space, such a line of thinking begs the further question, "So… what exactly was this infinite god of yours doing for the millions, no, billions, actually, trillions of gazillions of years before becoming so bored with nothingness that He finally decided to create an average planet near an average star on the edge of an average galaxy, just for the supremely amazing… *you?*"

Indeed, looking back at the first few words of the Bible, "In the beginning, God created…", one might logically ask, "Which god, exactly? Where did he/she/it come from, and why?" Unpacking these questions further, these basic questions are not only appropriate to be asked of god(s) of the Christian Bible, but of the many, many gods that predated *any* of the Judaic texts - many of which are even referenced by the "one true God" who just happens to go by the very telling name, Jealous. Believing the Bible to be true, an honest reader has no choice but to concede that, according to scripture, not only did countless other gods predate the Abrahamic god, but they were still being worshipped by "modern" man throughout the gestation of Judaism, Christianity and yes - Islam. But a reader must also be willing to recognize that had it not been for mankind's invention of ships capable of crossing oceans in search for gold, this "one true God" would likely have never been known to the entire western hemisphere of "savages." Suddenly the idea of an omnipresent God seems much less self-evident and much more targeted to address the local geopolitical needs of ancient Mesopotamia that were no longer being adequately fulfilled by the gods of earlier machinations.

So, then - who created *all* of these gods? It has taken several years away from ministry and the church for me to recognize the answer is actually quite simple - as with the oldest deities that are now long forgotten, the latest supernatural beings of modern religions are just another, (perhaps the last)

of a long line of gods brought to life by the imaginations of those searching for a deeper understanding of this terrifying thing we call life on earth. Who created the countless gods of countless traditions that have scattered the globe as long as mankind? By the end of the book, I hope the answer to that question will be painfully obvious.

I should state for those concerned by my cynicism, it's not like I never looked for God. I spent decades looking in church, reading His Word, asking for His forgiveness, singing His praises, eating the savior's flesh, preaching about His "love" for us… Heck, when I felt like I couldn't find Him within the constructs of church life, I'd hike alone through hundreds of miles of mountains, forests, and deserts in search of any empirical sign of a self-evident creator that wanted a personal relationship with me. Many miles were passed deep in prayer with an open mind and searching heart. Can you guess how many times I came to face to face with unimpeachable signs of a self-evident creator? I bet you can… Not once have I had the pleasure of engaging conversations with burning bushes, serpents, or donkeys. (Trust me, I've tried.) Why was I not worthy of an omnipresent God's presence in my life? What could I have been doing wrong all this time?

It has been through my own search for meaning that I've come to better recognize what these underlying questions are really getting at; how the origin of everything relates to *us*, personally, and what it all means for our place in a universe so deeply infinite of time and space that it is almost impossible to comprehend. In short, we have shaped the entire cosmos to reward our own narcissistic hubris. I had my own "aha" moment a few years ago when I caught the tail end of an interview as the guest gently challenged the host's self-indulgent notions:

> *"The entire universe doesn't exist just so you can be happy."*

Ouch! This was quite a departure from the standard Christian teaching that Jesus came to die for *me*! His torturous and bloody death was because of *my* sins, *mine*! And, most importantly, soon He'll be coming back for *me, me, me!* I put this statement onto a piece of tape at the base of my bathroom mirror - a great daily reminder that try as I might to convince myself (and others) to the contrary, I'm sadly not the apple of the universe's eye.

When it comes to gods and monsters, Anne Lamott, one of my favorite Christian authors gets to the heart of the issue quite quickly:

> *"You can safely assume you've created God in your own image when it turns out that He hates all the same people you do."*

It is in this vein that I've also come to the realization that there is nothing 'monotheistic' about any religion that is dependent upon an unwavering silent and absentee deity. That is to say, for any given religion, there appear to be as many gods (and monsters) as there are followers. Billions of followers beget billions of gods; each strangely (or dare I say conveniently) matching whatever checkboxes the follower is looking to fill for their deity du jour (requirements subject to change without notice). The only thing these countless gods seem to have in common is their startling inability to speak for themselves - a convenient silence that allows followers to further mold their personalized masters to the will of their own imaginations (and personal agendas).

In the case of the chicken or the egg, I've grown inclined to trust the research cited by my table-toppling friend who holds a PhD in biology. As for the genesis of gods and monsters, my thoughts on the matter have evolved significantly over the years to those of a devout creationist; it is *we* who create the gods in our own images. Ah, but the creative beings that we are, we couldn't stop there, our gods would need to be endlessly modified in order to fulfill our most primal needs and justify our darkest deeds for which we'd rather not be held personally responsible. So, then - who or what exactly are worshippers worshipping? The same self-evident omnipresent creator of the universe, or possibly, selectively benevolent boogey man of their own creation? When it comes to the creation of celestial super villains, just take a look in the mirror.

Critics of religious apologists often lament that, "they just act like they have all the answers." How does a Christian know their God created the universe? Because the Bible tells them so, silly! While there is certainly much evidence to the claim that many fundamentalists choose to live by a presuppositionalistic 'one book' philosophy when it comes to history, science, philosophy, and ethics, I can't help but acknowledge that it goes a bit deeper than that. Religionists are not alone in their apprehension to admit being wrong about anything. As a result, the willingness to even entertain challenging, or simply new questions often takes a back seat to the need to defend the "right" (old) answers, no matter how demonstrably lacking in evidence or fatally flawed in logic they may be. This phenomena is not limited to a Christian's argument against the views of an atheist, but often more vigorously with God's other followers. For evidence of this fracture, look no further than the tens of thousands of denominations and sects that continue to flow from the firehose of disagreements over the

interpretations of the only "Good Book" left behind by the one and only *true* God.

As I find myself stepping further away from religion, the less interested I've become in making sure everyone has the same answers. Instead, I find myself more and more drawn to people who are addicted to asking questions to begin with, those who remain open to answers that might challenge the very foundations of what they've accepted as "truth" throughout their entire lives - positions possibly cultivated from seeds planted at a very young age and perpetuated by regular reinforcement within the constructs of a religion chosen for them by their ancestors. In that spirit, this book isn't intended to tell you *what* to think, but to simply invite and encourage you *to* think - for yourself, away from the trappings of church and apologists all too eager to explain the latest interpretation of "what Jesus really meant." I invite you to join me as we illustrate a few of the questions I've been grappling with since re-investigating the Bible from a different perspective after leaving a life of full time ministry as a once devout Christian, not the least of which is... the *origin* of God. Welcome!

www.AwkwardMomentsBible.com/ChickenOrEgg

A Salivary Celebration

In our first book we touched on the story of a 600 year-old man who, without any previous boatbuilding experience, spent 120 years to construct an enormous wooden ship that would be be filled with the countless animals needed to repopulate the earth following the disastrous wrath of the most temperamental supernatural parent in history. For just a moment, though, please try to ignore the seemingly impossible task of building such a craft and stocking it with enough supplies required for the care and feeding of millions (if not billions) of animals that would inhabit the homemade superyacht for over a year. Instead, consider this particular passage of scripture and what took place immediately *after* the waters receded and the doors opened.

Just when you thought it was safe to step foot back on land, it's time for another illogically senseless slaughter! Call me crazy, but if I was now over 700 years old and had just gone through all the

trouble of saving a representative sampling of each species from a global flood, the very first order of business might *not* be to sacrifice the very animals I just worked so hard to rescue in the first place! But an ever deeper absurdity is a recurring theme of dominionism in the Bible that I have come to find not only primitive but immoral:

> *"All the animals of the earth, all the birds of the sky, all the small animals that scurry along the ground, and all the fish in the sea will look on you with **fear and terror**. I have placed them in your power."* Genesis 9:2

Because, sure - that's what every abused kid living in fear of an unseen God really needs, a puppy of his very own upon which to display his own god-given dominion over "lesser" beings - animals, slaves, wives... "Fear me, Spot! I'll show you who's boss!" Sadly, it should come as no surprise that a pastor in Alabama recently used the above passage to justify purposefully starving his own dog as part of a video teaching series on man's dominionship (not to be confused with stewardship) over all animals.

Say what you want about responsible hunters, at least they feed their families with animals that didn't spend their lives trapped in a cage or walked on a leash, lorded over with the "fear and terror" granted by the Lord. God, on the other hand? He just likes to open the cage for the "sweet smell" of burning sacrificial flesh from time to time. Awesome...

(Don't worry - there will be more on the ritualistic slaughter of animals a little later in the book.)

www.AwkwardMomentsBible.com/GodsBBQ

Assisted Living

969 years? Sweet candy Jesus, how exactly did that work? Did the aging of the earliest humans progress so slowly that on their 500th birthday, they would appear to be in their 50's by modern standards? Or, did they continue to age as their body deteriorated further and further until there was nothing left but a sagging bag of waste with eyelashes, just wishing that every breath would be their last? Or, was this all just a misunderstanding on the language used to describe the passage of time - years equal months, centuries equal years, etc... Or, is it at all possible that such extraordinary ages found in Genesis are more in line with the equally

grandiose mythologies involving a talking serpent or mighty ark found in nearby chapters?

Why don't modern humans live this long, you might ask? It's not cancer or diabetes or heart disease, silly! It should not be surprising that many Christians do indeed believe that back in the day, average people lived almost one thousand actual, trip-around-the-sun, calendar years. According to fundamentalist apologists who haven't turned their backs on "Biblical understanding," the cause for our modern premature death is the one ailment for which only Christianity offers a cure: SIN.

Sure, you might live 1/10th as long as Methuselah, but that's nothing compared to living for eternity with the guy who created heaven! (Sure, He also created hell, but we'll get to that later.)

Many apologists appear to caution readers against looking for any proof of Methuselah's unbelievable longevity. Why? Is it because such logical pursuits might also lead one to further ask what proof exists for all of the other other extraordinary Biblical claims? Critical thinking - a slippery slope, indeed!

www.AwkwardMomentsBible.com/OldestMan

The Prophet Of Profitable Penises

In recent years female genital mutilation has made the headlines and received the rightful shock and condemnation it deserves from rational citizens around the globe. The bizarre and barbaric practice is luckily so rare that hardly anybody even knew it existed, hidden in remote corners of the world. That is, until self-described "persecuted" Christians began to exploit the rare practice as another way to show the savagery of "radical" Islam. Ahh, yes - the ironic superiority complex of one amnesiac cult passing judgment on the largely disavowed acts of another.

But, why the selective outrage and condemnation? Simply put, the religion, methods, and gender aren't in line with their own normalized *values*, those based largely on the beliefs and practice of blood rituals of a slightly earlier iteration of Abrahamic tradition. Take one of these "values," for example; when it comes to the wholesale genital mutilation of entire generations of un-consenting infants - look no further than the multi-billion dollar industry of male infant circumcision right

here in the United States. Approximately 80% of American men are circumcised, compared to only 10% of Europeans. Why? Because… In God We Trust, dammit! (It also probably doesn't hurt that the industry happens to generate around $240 million from over a million operations every year.)

But, ask yourself - would male circumcision even be a "thing" today if not for an eccentric prophet who claimed to be hearing voices when he got caught in his tent with a naked young boy… and a knife? When God first made his covenant with Abraham, He clearly showed no interest in preventing HPV, reducing the rate of penile cancer, or potentially pleasing a baby's future sexual partners who might prefer their lovers to be "cut." After all, back in the day, gonorrhea wasn't believed to be the result of yet-to-be-discovered germs, but… demons! Naturally, according to the Bible, God made innocent babies so perfectly in His image that His first order of business was *obviously* to standardize genital mutilation as the visible sign of a child's "relationship" with a god he's never met.

Yes, I said it - genital mutilation, a cruel and immoral act regardless of gender or religion.

For those who would like to dismiss any criticism of male genital mutilation because of "medical benefits" like a 10% reduction of penile cancer that only affects 1-in-10,000 men (resulting in a literal 1-in-1,000,000 chance of benefit), I'd just ask why serious consideration isn't given to use a similar operation with a nearly 100% success rate in curbing an aggressive cancer that affects 1-in-6 women? Is the idea of infant mastectomies, without several centuries of normalized tradition not morally and ethically abhorrent? Of course it is - just like God's alleged covenant with Abraham. Could similar arguments not be made concerning the claimed benefits of circumcision vs. basic soap-and-water hygiene in efforts to combat bacteria found in foreskin? Are similar bacteria not just as readily present in the folds of the female labia? And, hell - don't even get me started on certain orthodox mohels who, to this day, infect babies with herpes by sucking the blood from freshly cut penises using their bare mouths! Ahh, religious freedoms...

But, who cares - right? Sure, I'll never pee straight as a result of how my infant circumcision scar "healed" and will always lack about a third of the sexual response resulting from the sensitive nerve endings that were once found in that little ring of flesh, but, whatevs - circumcision is totally normal(ized), right? (At least, in the evangelical United States where circumcision rates are far greater than any other "civilized" country.)

www.AwkwardMomentsBible.com/ProphetMGM

The Original Minions

Here we see Moses returning to his followers at the foot of the great Mt. Sinai - a geographical marvel of such historical and cultural significance to all Abrahamic religions that nobody throughout history has ever been able to prove where it might be located. Though indeed, many hotels, tour guides, and visitor bureaus have reaped huge profits by claiming that their particularly unimpressive pile of random rocks is the "real" Mt. Sinai. As a side note, isn't it interesting how such important relics of religious history tend to go missing without a moment's notice, whether as small as Joseph Smith's magic hat or as large as Moses' magic mountain? On the other hand, many proudly claim to have in their possession the authentic foreskin of Christ's circumcision. Sigh...

Returning from his suspiciously mandated "alone time" with the Lord, Moses shares the new list of rules and regulations found in the Book of The Covenant with his followers. The extensive list begins in Exodus 20, a chapter to which many modern Bibles would later *insert* the purely *editorial* label, *The Ten Commandments* - a title *never* affirmed by God nor His Word. (We'll be discussing the *actual* Ten Commandments in a moment.)

This ambiguous volume of rules (far more than ten) seems to never end, rambling on and on to include great detail on the construction of altars, guarantees against miscarriages, laws surrounding the sale of personal property such as daughters and oxen, and even helpful party-planning tips on the proper celebration of important festivals. Of course, as has come to be expected of the Lord's endless laws, the whole thing eventually wraps up with God's graphically detailed promises of deadly wrath against any tribes that might stand in Moses' way.

Without question, Moses' followers are quick to accept all of the new rules undeniably couriered from God by their holy middleman (a nice parlor trick later re-used by the likes of Joseph Smith, L. Ron Hubbard, and, well…Jesus). Apparently not concerned by how many of these regulations happen to be advantageous to Moses and the other priests, the doe-eyed followers agree to the new contracts of human slavery, death penalties for children, the price of a rape victim, and proper disposal of those accused of witchcraft.

How do they sign the covenant, you might ask? By conducting a charming little blood ritual that requires the slaughter of animals and splattering of their blood among the crowds of followers gathered before the Lord's holy altar. Of course, naturally...

Tell me again how Abrahamic religions were not born of tribalistic blood cults? The only reason such practices eventually fell out of favor in most modern parts of the world is because of secular progress rejecting such idiocy from the public square. Of course, it should be noted that certain sects around the world can still be found sacrificing animals to please their gods, a practice which the majority of modern Christians would attribute to... witchcraft!

www.AwkwardMomentsBible.com/BloodyMinions

The Golden... Cleansing

Am I missing something? Did Moses not just require his blood-drenched followers to agree to God's rule against KILLING people? Oh, unless God tells him to murder his own tribe? Right, got it - certainly no opportunity for abuse in that arrangement, is there?

This is one of those charming little Bible stories that is equaled in its ridiculousness only by its proof of man-made origins. Isn't it strange how neither Moses nor God found it necessary to hold Aaron to the same level of accountability as his followers who were forced to kill their own kin? Aaron, the very man who broke the rules he had just agreed to in order to construct the golden calf to worship? No sword or plague for him - just convenient nepotism for the brother of the "prophet" who announced the rules to begin with. Speaking of breaking the rules - what about Moses literally breaking the rules to pieces all over the ground? It's almost as if there were no God involved in Moses' little scheme at all. Likewise, the idea of selective hypocrisy among clergy appears to be nothing new.

Doesn't it also seem a little counterintuitive for God (and Moses) to call for the slaughter of the very people they just went out of their way to rescue from Egypt in the first place? Sooner or later, if they keep killing everyone they've rescued, nobody will be left in the tribe of Israel! Except, of course, Moses and his own newly-affluent family members. (More on God's ongoing switch-a-roos coming up.)

More troubling than the expected nepotism is how throughout the chapters surrounding Mt. Sinai, Moses is eager to remind his followers of the same sado-masochistic requirement expected of modern Christians today - the ability to demonstrate their compulsory love to the same god they are regularly instructed to fear. Though, I should mention the early Jews were able to achieve this level of duplicitous devotion without all of the promises of heaven and threats of hell, new arguments made so persuasively to Christians by Jesus himself.

www.AwkwardMomentsBible.com/GoldenCleansing

The *Real* Ten Commandments™

Call me a Biblical literalist, but when Christians campaign to have the Ten Commandments on display in every school and courthouse in America, I'd like to think they'd demand using the *only* set of rules the Bible explicitly refers to as *The* Ten Commandments - the longwinded set of rules found in Exodus 34:27-28, summarized (greatly) here for your reading pleasure:

1. Never make a treaty with other nations, you must destroy their culture and not worship any other gods because even the Lord's name is Jealous.

2. Never make a treaty with other nations or their wicked women will seduce your sons to commit adultery against Me by worshiping other gods. No metal gods either.

3. Once a year celebrate the Passover and don't eat yeast for a week.

4. Every firstborn animal belongs to the Lord [clergy]. You may buy it back if you can afford it. Otherwise, you must kill it. Though, every firstborn son *must* be bought back from the Lord.

5. Nobody may appear before the Lord [clergy] without an offering. (Naturally...)

6. Work for six days, rest on the seventh. (No, seriously - if you get caught working you'll be put to death. Why? Because... God.)

7. Celebrate the harvests of the first and final crops. Also, three times each year every man must appear before the Lord while He conquers all the other nations for you. (World domination... got it.)

8. Don't mix blood and yeast in your offerings to the Lord [clergy]. Also, no leftovers please...

9. The best crops of the first harvest must be given to the House Of The Lord [clergy].

10. Don't boil a kid in its mother's milk. (Because...? Well, just trust me - it's nasty.)

These rules are obviously much more important to incude in the official Top-10 list than any laws against, say... rape, slavery, or child abuse. Lucky for Moses and Aaron, "thou shall not murder" went missing from the list just in time for their massacre ordained by God.

Why are all of these laws involving treaty bans and offerings suddenly so important? It might have something to do with this all just being superstitious witchcraft mixed with nationalistic edicts promoting a drive for Jewish domination/supremacy while, of coure, simultaneously filling church offers with an unending stream of valuable offerings.

Regardless, I'd love to see these on a school lawn.

www.AwkwardMomentsBible.com/Real10

Deny The Defects!

Can you imagine driving past a church to see the words, "Hunchbacks Not Welcome" in big block letters across their roadside sign? Of course not! Yet, on more than one occasion in ministry , I came across a church that proudly displayed an official (looking) blue handicap sign close to the entrance with the words "Soon To Be Healed." Are these signs actually available at Christian supply stores? I do remember that at least one of these churches had the foresight and budget to put the cheesy sign in a space next to an actual handicapped spot, but then lacked any accessible ramps or doors to welcome those in wheelchairs or requiring a walker. I mean...

If you were to do a Google search for "church + disability" you'd find a treasure trove of recent sermons, articles, and even entire books about the church's responsibility toward people with special needs. It should be noted that all of this content shares a common theme - how the church needs to *change* in order to become more welcoming and accommodating to the "defects" of the world. So prevalent are these modern writings that one has to look a bit more closely to see how the church historically treated members of society who, not so long ago, were hidden away in attics and basements, shame-inducing embarrassments to kept away from the altar of the family church. Ahh, but with secular progress comes sacred re-interpretation (and self-righteous amnesia).

Isn't it interesting how all organized religions evolve over the centuries in search of wider audiences? In earlier times, someone with simple acne wouldn't have even been allowed in the temple. Sure, they could pray to the Lord, just not in public. Mercifully, though - they were still allowed to tithe. Fast forward to modern day and churches are suddenly going out of their way to accommodate any "special needs" that might cross their threshold. Sadly, at times crossing the line from earnest accommodation to blatant exploitation. It seems that nearly every church graces its doorstep these days with a *very* special greeter, indeed. Someone suffering with just enough of a visible disability (but not enough to disgust fellow congregants) that they should be given the uniform of a mascot, proof of their church's awesome inclusive atmosphere. At least, during business hours, that is.

Though, if you put it in the proper Biblical context, this opportunistically self-serving street theater feels just about right. After all, according to the Bible, how many people did Jesus heal of horrible afflictions? Now, how many did He invite to travel along as one of His disciples? Heck, the Bible rarely even tells us their names! Disabled, thus desirable. Yet - once any possible exploitation had been exhausted, ultimately disposable.

I hate to be so cynical, but I say this as a recovering ministry leader who was also the step-father of a very photogenic child who happened to be afflicted with very visible physical disabilities - the cute crippled kid who was often recruited to 'play the part' for various Christian organizations in need of a P.R. boost in the accessibility department.

My family once visited a fairly charismatic church and found a pastor with a slightly different take on the "defects" of the Bible.

"It breaks my heart to see people with disabilities around our city," he said. "These folks need to get in here and be healed. Look around to the people next to you. None of you can even remember the

afflictions you were suffering with before you walked through those doors. God wants to heal your friends and neighbors just like He healed each and every one of you. All they have to do is ask. The only thing standing in the way of healing is not having enough faith in Christ, Jesus. Look around you!"

Uh... what?!?! Was he earnestly suggesting that if I looked to my left, I'd see a perfectly healthy woman who once had cerebral palsy, so healed from her infirmities that even she wouldn't remember suffering from a lifetime of spastic paralysis? Well, I did look around. He was right - I didn't see anyone with disabilities, just congregants creepily nodding at one another as if this were some sort of a real thing. By the time I looked the other direction, my wife was already halfway out the door of the sanctuary. I found her in the children's wing, clearly doing her best to *show* how she wasn't going to lose her cool while our kids gathered their things.

"I'm sorry you won't be able to stay for the entire service," the assistant teacher said nicely. "Is there a problem?"

"Your pastor is a disgusting human being," my wife half-shouted. "That's the problem!" So much for staying calm.

"Well, I never! Excuse me?" Wide-eyed, the poor volunteer became quite flustered and defensive. After all, this was her church, her turf.

"Our daughter already has to overcome all of the physical, mental, and social hurdles that go along with her disability. But, according to that fruitcake in there, if her faith isn't enough to re-route nerve endings, re-grow muscle, and replace brain tissue that has been missing since birth - that will be her fault, too?" Then, almost comically, "SHAME!"

Though we'd divorce years later, I'll always have a great deal of admiration and appreciation for my ex-wife's unrelenting passion to advocate for those who might lack the means to advocate for themselves. If only we all had such resolve.

Obviously not all churches exploit those with special needs in order to pat themselves on the back in public. Many churches are really doing it right - giving opportunity for community, employment, and even housing where few other options might exist for people living with disabilities. Sadly, if we are to acknowledge the inclusion modern churches have evolved to offer the "defects" of the world, we must also acknowledge that this humanistic generosity is only made possible *despite* the Bible, not because of it. After all, it was God, not I, who said, "they will *defile* my holy places." As such, I'll likely always find it difficult to accept the modern church's revisionist high-road concerning "defects."

www.AwkwardMomentsBible.com/Defects

Sticks & Stones

Did you know that anytime a stone sees a man picking up a stick, it checks its calendar for the day of the week in order to decide whether or not to magically propel itself at the man's temple with enough force to crack his skull and cause immediate death? No? Of course not - that would be crazy! It's just a rock, an inanimate object free of any such idiocy! After all, it takes a person armed with the zeal of God's wrath to kill another human being over something as stupid as doing chores on the wrong day of the week.

Sticks and stones may break my bones, 'cuz the Bible tells others to throw them. Ahh, religion - what could possibly go wrong? (Next verse, please...)

www.AwkwardMomentsBible.com/SticksStones

God's Enemies = My Enemies

I've been asked a number of times why we rarely cover the Bible's various instructions to murder people of other faiths, be it strangers from far-off lands or members of one's own family. I guess it has been a matter of *conditioned* respect – not wanting to upset Christian readers by illuminating some of the darkest roots of violent totalitarianism found in the sacred texts of Judaism, Islam, and... Christianity. In truth, just as Christians avoid the subject to protect their faith, I likely avoided the subject to protect my brand. As a Christian, I became a master of changing the subject or playing the "context" card any time an awkward subject came up. Out of sight, out of mind – hide it in the closet, don't talk about it, and it's almost as if it doesn't actually exist. The problem is, playing ostrich doesn't change reality.

How is this passage still relevant today? It's not just radical Muslims who use the fear inspired by their religion to intimidate others. As it turns out, not all Christians are as "meek and mild" as their Christ is generally portrayed. A couple of years ago, this passage made several appearances in a series of death threats sent to my home address - just days before I was scheduled to speak at a national conference. Did I think the author of such stupid letters would be able to tear themselves away from their mother's basement long enough to carry out such insidious threats? Probably not. On the other hand, in speaking with event organizers and criminal investigators, everyone agreed that there was enough precedent of someone being willing to kill others in order for their god to be taken seriously. In the end, due to the last-minute timing and shared concerns over security for others, I decided to cancel my appearance and avoid becoming a distraction to the organizers, speakers, and attendees.

But, death threats over irreverently illustrated books of real Bible stories? If you think the threats worked to silence me, you'd be wrong. All they did was bring light to the fact that such insanity still exists today - as covered through a series of articles, interviews, podcasts, and blogs featuring attendees showing their non-silenced solidarity by wearing badges that read, *"Hello, my name is Horus Gilgamesh"* throughout the conference. In the end, the situation also helped me re-think my position of showing "respect" for various lesser-known Biblical concepts that deserve nothing but disdain. After all, what "respect" should any decent society show for religions built upon sacred texts that include any prescriptions of violence and death to anyone with differing views? I'd argue... none.

From Genesis to Revelation, there are many Bible passages that remain completely unknown by the average believer, largely because they are completely avoided by their pastors. Yet, these same verses are often clung to as law by the most militant fundamentalists and end-times apocalyptisists with their unquenchable thirst to see God's wrath carried out on others. Please understand – the Bible is not referring to capital punishment as a result of a person's actions, but premeditated murder because of their beliefs. The harshest of penalties for the most innocent of thought-crimes - the deadly offense of thinking for oneself.

Even as a Christian, when asked rhetorically whether I'd be willing to kill for God, my answer then was the same as it is now – "If God really wants them dead, let Him do his His own dirty work!" Sadly, to some, this would just be further proof that I was never a "true" Christian to begin with. I would also caution more progressive Christians to not dismiss such prescriptions as mere remnants of tribal warfare that predated the "new" (and unimproved) covenant offered by Jesus. We'll be discussing "death to heretics" in more detail a

little later as we move to the New Testament. Nonetheless, conversations about these passages are still quite relevant and necessary today.

Of course, none of this addresses the stealthy problem of God's followers' recurring perception and/or justification that *their* enemies are actually *His* enemies. After all, if not His vociferous followers, who speaks on behalf of this supremely speechless being? It doesn't take swords and death threats for a religious majority to largely silence, control, and oppress the masses. It only takes *perceived* authority applied into real *power* through, for example, an overwhelming majority in both houses of Congress, The White House, and The Supreme Court. (But, oh - the *'persecution!'* Right.)

For those who'd hope to dismiss the more troublesome teachings of the Old Testament as "no longer relevant" in modern society, one might simply point out that the vandalism against mosques and violence against Muslims that has increased exponentially in the United States following the 2016 election has not been carried out by atheists and agnostics, but card-carrying Christians armed with the authority of scripture. Imagine no religion? If only we were allowed...

www.AwkwardMomentsBible.com/GodsHelpers

Severed Justice

For a book that preaches "eye for an eye" retribution, you've got to wonder what would happen if it were a man who seized a woman by her genitals. Would he lose his hand? Uh... nope. According to the Good Book, a man's "punishment" for brutally raping a child is to be "forced" to keep her as a child bride, a carefully selected victim, now his prized possession for all eternity to do with whatever he pleases. Yet, if a woman has the audacity to break up a fight and her hand touches an assailant's genitals - she loses her entire hand? Talk about punitive, gee-zus!

What if she was literally saving her husband's life and defending her children? What if she was using the only "trick" she could think of to break the grasp of a strong assailant holding a knife to her husband's throat while his henchmen kidnapped her children into slavery? Wouldn't she be hailed as a hero for courageously putting her own life in

danger to save her family from harm? Nope - off with the hand! And don't just let her punishment stop there - let her stump serve as a reminder to other women that God's laws show no mercy! (And people wonder how misogyny has been so easily perpetuated by Abrahamic cultures?)

In his book *Is God A Moral Monster?* (Baker, 2011), Paul Copan employs a heaping dose of linguistic analysis to this passage in order to suggest that the original Hebrew may have actually called for the woman's pubic hair to be removed, not her hand. Why? Because having her lady bits exposed and shaved publicly in the town square would have been much more shameful and humiliating than the mere pain and lifetime of disability that comes from a severed limb. While certainly a perverse scene of public pubic punishment, I can't help but feel that it might be the wishful thinking of a theologian armed with a troubled imagination.

First, does this alternative interpretation really make the passage any more palatable, morally? Second, it was still the grotesquely traumatic and inequitable treatment of a woman that the Lord's appointed leaders eventually agreed upon as an appropriate punishment for touching the forbidden fruit. Finally, and perhaps most importantly, in a day that scholars are still arguing whether a passage instructs to "cut off her hand" vs. "remove her pubic hair" countless pastors and apologists proudly claim to know exactly "what Jesus really meant." Please...

In either case, hands or pubes, this is one of the many Biblical laws that *should* lead its readers to ask: which is more likely - the loving master of the universe dolling out capriciously punitive punishments against only *half* of His creation - or maybe - just maybe, Moses enjoyed the mighty view from atop his manmade tower of misogynistic patriarchy, instituting new laws to keep it that way?

www.AwkwardMomentsBible.com/HandJob

Daddy's Little Girl

This short and simple story gets to the point quickly without needing a decoder ring for proper interpretation. During a foxhole moment, Japbeth made a deal with God to exchange his life for that of his very own daughter, promising to carry out the murder himself. (No, really...)

Now, before you claim that God somehow didn't actually condone Japheth's killing of his innocent daughter (as many apologists jump through all sorts of exegetical hoops to attempt), let me just remind you that it was God who willingly accepted the bribe without any objection and, according to the Bible, made good on His end of the bargain by slaughtering Japbeth's enemies. Most importantly, God never stopped, nor later rebuked Japheth for killing his own daughter. **Period.**

As a side note, one might ask if other non-supernatural factors may have contributed to the change in events that led to Japbeth's victory over the opposing troops. Maybe they simply ran out of weapons? Maybe they received orders to report to a more pressing battle elsewhere? Maybe they became weakened with amoebic dysentery? Maybe, just maybe, there were no sacrificed daughters necessary to achieve victory? Nah!

If this story is not explicitly intended to inspire a devout reader to follow Japheth's level of conviction in making good on superstitious promises to their unseen rainmakers, please - tell me what this story is *really* about.

I'll wait.

Tic-toc. Tic-toc.

Still waiting...

www.AwkwardMomentsBible.com/DaddyIssues

Golden Hemorrhoids

Do you remember those extremely important "Ten" Commandments that Moses brought down from on high? No, not the first ones he smashed, silly - the Real Ten Commandments - the ones nobody seems to know anything about. As it turns out, those rules were actually top secret, only meant to be viewed by God's "chosen ones" (du jour). If anybody else tried to read God's rules-to-live-by, they would surely die! (Or, maybe they'd just get... hemorrhoids? Same, same, I guess.)

Great plan, God. I mean, if it were me and I wanted all of the people on earth to follow such important rules, maybe I'd just publish them and distribute them freely. Hell, maybe I'd even perform a cool trick like writing them in the clouds and turning them into a funky rhyming ditty to make them easier to remember. Ah, but no - hide the rules

of the universe inside the Ark of the Covenant under penalty of death (or hemorrhoids) to any who might even attempt to see the alleged tablets of truth. A truly genius strategy for the efficient dissemination of and compulsory compliance with concepts as groundbreaking as, "Don't mix blood with yeast in the offering dish!" Hmm... I can't imagine why nobody seems to care about the rules.

It's almost as if rational and moral adults never needed to see such laws in the first place. It's almost as if it was only the religionists who needed to rely on nationalistic instructions banning the influence of other nations inside their borders.

But, magic golden hemorrhoids? Cool.

www.AwkwardMomentsBible.com/GoldenH

My Cherub & Me

Let's forget about the smoke pouring from God's nostrils as He throws lightning and arrows from atop an adorable cherub. Nobody actually believes this nonsense, do they? Oh... right.

Nevertheless, let's examine the original author's psyche for just a moment, taking a look at one theme that has also become commonplace among many modern Christians. To repeat a phrase often used by my family to describe someone with an overly active ego and sense of self-importance, "David was pretty happy with the way he turned out, wasn't he?"

And why wouldn't he be? He had convinced himself, no, really - David actually convinced himself that God, the creator of the entire universe was always standing by, ready to put everything else on hold whenever he needed a holy helping hand (usually in the form of a murderous rampage against his own enemies).

I mean, wow... Kanye has nothing on David.

Meanwhile, still today, Jews, Christians, and Muslims continue to wage wars with the firm belief that the same god just happens to be on *their* side of every battle. How exactly do they know this? I'm sure it has nothing to do with cultural indoctrination and systemic narcissism. *My* God and *me!*

www.AwkwardMomentsBible.com/MyCherub

Convenient Condescension

A suspicious stranger approaches your child from across the playground and just as you jump to their aid, you hear the verbal assault, "You are stupid! You're corrupt, and evil - nothing good will ever come of you!" Can you even imagine such a thing? How would you react?

What if an entire group of complete strangers was reduced to, "stand for nothing, believe in nothing, and many are good for nothing"? That's exactly what Bill Donohue, president of The Catholic League claimed in an official June 2016 press release - all because a group of "nobodies" (well known politicians, scientists, entertainers, and authors) joined together for a sequel to the popular Reason Rally in Washington D.C.. *Good for nothing?* Who could even make such an arrogant claim?

Lastly, imagine an influential religious leader using this scripture to justify the murder of their longtime friend and colleague. As a matter of fact, that's exactly what John Calvin, major leader of the Protestant Reformation did when a fellow Bible scholar had the audacity to scribble a few notes of critique in the margin of Calvin's seminal work, *Institutes of the Christian Religion.* Calvin later used this "fool hath said" passage to justify having Michael Servetus arrested, tried, and *roasted* alive by the Spanish Inquisition. Calvin was so convinced of a Christian's authority over others that he later boasted:

"Many people have accused me of such ferocious cruelty that I would like to kill again the man that I have destroyed. Not only am I indifferent to their comments, I rejoice in the fact that they spit in my face."

Think about that for a moment… John Calvin, father of the Reformation - a proudly murderous zealot if ever there was. (And namesake of a highly respected Christian university.)

When you take even a moment to consider the harm inflicted by the Bible's "worth nothing" ideologies, it's not difficult to understand why so many choose to reject the myopic superiority complex enjoyed by those who claim such authority as coming conveniently from their particular god. Such self-prescribed power is the sort of stuff bullies rely on to marginalize, intimidate, and oppress others. One doesn't have to look too closely at the rhetoric being used by today's most prominent Christian leaders to imagine such terms as "worthless" or "good for nothing" being levied to attack the gay atheist scientist whose grave is depicted in this illustration.

So, the next time someone tries to reduce you with such claims, try to have pity. Remember, your accuser was likely indoctrinated as a child to believe the same "good for nothingness" of themselves, never afforded the simple dignity of discovering their own self worth.

While it may be easy to imagine others uttering such demoralizing hatred toward their fellow man, just imagine being trapped in a shell of your potential self, programmed to, in the image of God, only make yourself greater and greater by requiring others to become lesser and lesser... in *your* eyes. If anything, this Psalm perfectly underscores one of the more troubling tenets that must be embraced by the aspiring Christian - that you, yourself, are a "worthless no-good" loser if you even question the existence of the almighty God. But, in order to "receive" Him, you must simultaneously embrace that you were born a broken "worthless no-good" wretch who doesn't deserve Him in the first place. A classic Catch-22 lose-lose scenario for the human psyche that *only* religion could provide.

When you understand the self-loathing it takes to accept such terms, either willingly, or through no fault of your own as a malleable child, it is easier to understand how some Christians find it almost compulsively easy to say something so wretched to a child of their own, or a friend, or perfect stranger. One of the greatest liberations to come out of my eventual rejection of Christianity was the decision to no longer allow anyone to speak to me in such hateful ways and I'd encourage you to incorporate similar protections against those who seek to diminish and demean others in their quest to empower and elevate themselves, if only in their own eyes. Have pity...

Spoiler Alert: Jesus also made similar claims against anyone who wouldn't follow Him, even His own disciples and family members. In real life, if you have to rely on threats and bullying tactics to win friends and influence others, this doesn't make you powerful, but... pitiful.

www.AwkwardMomentsBible.com/HighHorse

God's Prophet or... Puppet?

My wife and I were on a train from New York to Washington D.C. when a man got out of his seat, walked to the head of the car, and began removing his clothes while giving an impassioned speech. The subject of his oratory, you might ask? He waxed poetic about alien slaves aboard UFO's that were being used to steal the earth's supply of gold in efforts to devalue our currency and drive down the cost of... waterbeds. Yep - alien slaves, gold mining, and discount waterbeds.

By the time the man was completely naked (and screaming), multiple transit authorities were already responding to emergency signals tripped by fellow passengers. As the nutty nudist was escorted out of our cabin, one could barely hear his final words behind a closing door, "Next they'll take your hot tubs - you'll see! Then you'll be sorry!"

We all glanced around the train at each other with looks of amused solidarity, "Can you believe that actually just happened?"

Meanwhile, on that same Sunday morning, billions of people gathered around the world to worship Jesus Christ, the Son of God! One might wonder how Christians have come to rest so confidently in their beliefs of the Messiah. Have they ever actually met this Jesus fellow? No, no - their beliefs are based largely in the ramblings of another naked man, one who wandered the streets naked for three years - the "great" prophet, Isaiah. I think there's a name for someone who walks around in their birthday suit while muttering endlessly about God's bloody wraths. Lazy? Dazey? Oh, wait - naked for three whole years? That's just:

*BATSH*T F***ING CRAZY!!!*

That's right, folks - without any actual evidence for the divinity of the self-described Messiah, Christians must regularly cite the words of *Isaiah*, the serial doomsday streaker, in order to prop up their beliefs as... *fact?* Imagine if Christians were expected to accept similarly generous credibility waivers for the claims of Scientology or Islam?

Almost every chapter of Isaiah is a warning of God's impending violent doom to be leveled against specific cities, or, even entire nations. Most of his threats can be summarized, "Hey, neighbor - God will kill you, you'll see!" Yet, nobody locked him up

for terrorism. When Isaiah spoke of a Messiah coming to take the place of the *one* true God, nobody locked him up for blasphemy. Heck, when he spoke of God murdering unicorns, nobody seemed to mind. In fact, if anything, they seemed to be wanting more from the "great" prophet. Why? Because Isaiah lived at a time when it was dangerous to challenge anyone who professed to be a mouthpiece for God. Nobody ever knew which mumbling flasher might have found favor with the powerful leaders of the day and questioning the wrong raving exhibitionist might prove to be downright deadly. And there lies the rub - when nobody is able to question those who claim to speak on behalf of the Lord of Laryngitis, well... anything is possible!

Fast forward a few hundred years and we find Jesus walking the streets, making outrageous claims of His own, often quoting many of the well known Messianic prophecies of the past as predictions of His own divinity. Imagine that - one self-appointed prophet quoting another self-appointed prophet as the proof of His own divinity. What are the odds, right? At least Jesus wasn't naked, but one must consider the original source.

There's only one problem. Even observant Jews, armed with the previously published works of the greatest Prophets who predicted the arrival of a coming Messiah - even they found the claims born of Isaiah's balls-out benders to be highly unconvincing. How could they not believe Jesus? He magically checked off all of the boxes of the previously created list that was provided to him at birth. He was Messiah, *made-to order.*

Unlike Isaiah who enjoyed the charmed life of an untouchable prophet, by the time Jesus repeatedly took ownership of the outrageous claims of the troubled nudist, authorities eventually did take notice. Though both scenes are quite sad in their own ways, I, for one, take the incident on the train and the crucifixion at Calvary as signs of society's progress - no longer willing to allow "because I said so" to be the final word of troubled preachers who threaten strangers with death, naked or not. It should also be noted that unlike back in Jesus' day, the man on the train likely received at least opportunities to address his mental health.

That said, if you hear of any new religions popping up that involve alien waterbed hoarding, please let me know!

www.AwkwardMomentsBible.com/PuppetProphet

Creator Of All

I recently went on a backpacking trip in the High Sierra with a Christian friend who kept remarking on the awe-inspiring landscape surrounding us. While dangling our legs over a granite cliff after sunset, the moon began to rise when he asked in a voice of tragic sincerity, "Can you believe that some people actually think this all happened randomly? By accident?"

I knew full well that I was being baited, but I decided to play along. "No, actually I can't believe that. I think most folks understand the difference between an 'accident' and the incredibly complex but increasingly explained forces at work in cosmology, biology, anthropology, geology, astronomy, physics, and even meteorology."

"Oh, please - none of that explains how it all came to be in the first place. Something can't come from nothing!"

"You mean, unless magic is involved? An invisible bearded man in white robes waves his hands and… poof! The Milky Way? But, actually, the latest discoveries in quantum mechanics and particle physics appear to suggest that something is always bound to eventually come from nothing. That is, until Christian 'scientists' keep moving the bar and changing the definition of what 'nothing' is." This was not the first time we'd had this conversation. "I mean, come on - our ancestors used to believe that earthquakes and volcanoes were the work of the god's angry hands. Now we have a bit better understanding of geology and plate tectonics, suddenly it's only folks like Pat Robertson who blame natural disasters on boys kissing other boys."

"Laugh all you want, but you can't have creation without a creator." Oh, snap!

"Except, well… what did the creator use to create everything in the first place? I can't remember the last time I saw a potter make a vase without starting with lumps of clay, a wheel, glazes, and a kiln."

"He's God! He CREATED it all to begin with!"

"From what?" The poor guy set his own trap.

"Nothing, I guess."

"Ahhh… so, it's perfectly acceptable if *He* creates *everything* from nothing?"

"Of course… He's God!" He was getting… excited.

"So, you'd rather believe in a wickedly capricious God, the creator of good AND evil who creates countless mutations of cancers to test the resolve of His own followers and created the geo-political landscape to spawn ISIS to chop off their heads?"

"God doesn't create evil!" Now he was a bit pissed.

"Then who does? Even God himself brags about creating evil."

"No He doesn't. Evil is the result of sin!"

"When we get back, you need to read Isaiah 45:7. But, what is sin, exactly? Can it be weighed, measured? Who defines it, using what criteria?"

"Oh, don't play dumb with me - sin is simply the result of our own brokenness."

"So… an invisible god not only creates everything from nothing, but He also creates an invisible sin that somehow produces evil."

"God didn't create sin, it is the result of our wickedness."

"Ahh, so even though God explicitly says that *He* is the creator of *all* things, good *and* evil, and evil is the result of sin, you aren't willing to accept and give *Him* credit for creating sin? Or, wait - are you calling the Biblical God, the creator of the universe, a… liar?"

"Oh, give it up already. God didn't create sin! Man did!"

"Funny, I kind of feel like if man ate an apple, it would just be an apple, right? That is, if it weren't for the mysterious ways of God forbidding it as a sin. If a man wore a cotton wool blend he'd never know it was a sin unless God told him so. What exactly about the Sabbath is so self evident that a man would know to not pick up sticks without offending the Lord?"

"Fine, but God didn't create sin - it just is!"

"Prove it!" I threw a granola bar at him and we got into our sleeping bags, continuing to bicker like an old married couple out under the stars.

But, back to the original point - if the Bible is to be believed, you can thank the Creator for His endless list of creations - good *and* evil, light *and* dark. You know, *all* the things - diarrhea, mayonnaise, Alex Jones, Florida… How capricious!

www.AwkwardMomentsBible.com/EvilCreator

Whale of a Tale

So… how much do you think ancient nearly-illiterate tribes really knew about the physiology of fantastic creatures of the sea (marine biology) - not to mention the minimum oxygen and water requirements necessary for an average man to survive for three days (human biology)? Did they think of a whale's blowhole as a snorkel that somehow filled its stomach with air, rather than filling its lungs? Did they think a whale's organs were the same relative size as humans', leaving room for a studio apartment complete with massive oxygen reserve tanks and fresh water to drink? Oh, that's right… to any thinking adult, this is obviously just a made up children's story. (That's why it's awkward that Jesus thinks it's true…)

Unfortunately for Christians, whenever leaders would ask Jesus for a "sign" (to prove that He was who/what He said He was), He'd deflect and remind them that Jonah was a real prophet who spent "three days and nights in the belly of a huge fish." Uh, so? *(Matthew 12:38-41, Luke 11:29-30,32)*

That's right folks, Jesus, an ancient apocalyptic preacher with a primitive understanding of human (and aquatic) biology actually believed that Jonah lived inside a "great fish" for three days and often relayed the story to others. No, not allegorically, not metaphorically, but… literally. In fact, He used this widely believed story to bolster His own prophetic status as He, Himself, was "greater than Jonah."

Sadly, many of Christ's similarly ignorant anti-science followers believe this story today. Literally. How, why? Because His absentee Daddy is magic, and it's right there in *the* book, silly!

Luckily, these sorts of Christians are of a fading minority, mostly spending their time building tax-free amusement parks in rural Kentucky in order to fleece equally ignorant members of literalist cults. On the other hand - if Christians no longer stand on the basis of Biblical truths - what *is* the foundation of their faith?

www.AwkwardMomentsBible.com/WhaleTale

Massacres, Made-To-Order

Christians dodged a bullet on June 12, 2016. They held their collective breath as initial reports described the massacre at a gay night club in Orlando where a lone gunman took the lives of 49 and wounded 53 others. Their hearts stopped as they jumped to the same silent conclusion, subconsciously preparing their response that, "no true Christian would ever…" Then, as if by a miracle from above, Christians across America breathed an enormous sigh of relief when, much to their surprise, the shooter wasn't a fellow Christian after all. Even better - it was the only enemy of their faith considered more dangerous than 'the gays' - a 'radical Islamic terrorist,' faithfully carrying out the very same death penalties many Christians often speak of, prescribed througout their own Bibles.

"Thank God," they whispered, "it wasn't one of us." Of course, deep down they knew they dodged a major bullet. Deep down they were relieved the shooter had been killed at the scene, sparing them having to witness the ironically hypocritical arguments of a Muslim being charged with crimes often hinted at, if not openly advocated for from the pulpit. Just imagine - a lengthy trial against religious extremism taking place in a courtroom bearing the forced motto, *In God We Trust*. "Thank God," indeed - a bullet narrowly dodged.

Make no mistake, these two passages of scripture are not obscure, out of context, or irrelevant in any way. They have been weaponized by powerful pastors, religious leaders, and politicians for centuries in their never-ending war against the LGBTQ+ community. These passages of both the Old Testament *and* New Testament have been preached as God's Law from the pews of the smallest local churches to the halls of the greatest power in our nation's capital. *Death to the gays…*

These well-known verses are not *only* the stuff of "fringe fanatics" waving "God Hates Fags" signs on the street corner, but they are also regularly preached by highly influential mainstream Christian leaders trusted by millions of followers - big celebrities like Dr. James Dobson, Franklin Graham, Pat Robertson and countless other modern clergy, authors, and scholars. These murderous verses are so often used to vilify the LGBTQ+ community that major news networks no longer even bother to report when they are shouted from the stage at political rallies where presidential candidates trip over themselves to compete for the crucial evangelical vote. Nothing to see here, folks - just more of the same, Christian leaders preaching death to gays. (It was no mistake that Senator Ted Cruz went on to win conservative states like Iowa, Texas, Kansas, Oklahoma, and Wisconsin just weeks after such an event.)

Christians were faced with an important choice on the morning of June 12, 2016. Some Christians sent thoughts and prayers while others praised the deaths and prayed for even more. Some Christians had the decency to stay silent in response while others vowed to continue their fight against marriage equality. Some Christians, 150 respected leaders to be exact, joined forces to sign a manifesto known as the Tennessee Statement, an unnecessary and redundant profession of Biblical principles involving gender, sexuality, and marriage. The document was created in large part to challenge all

homosexuality, transgenderism, and same-sex marriage as abominations against God's Laws (which, of course are greater than man's laws). It should come as no surprise that in the official "Scripture References" supplied with the document, you will find Leviticus 20:13 and Romans 1:32 right there, in bold print. To date over 20,000 have proudly signed this bold reminder of ancient divisiveness and the deadly punishments carried with it. On behalf of and with the support their countless fans and followers, they have all agreed, *"The penalty is death…"* (Christian Readers: Be very careful what you wish for and don't act so surprised when dangerous beliefs translate to deadly actions.)

The thing is, all of these pastors and politicians, joined by their flocks and fans, all have one thing in common - they profess to worship the same God who "inspired" this deadly drivel into print and daily life in the first place. While theologians continue their centuries-old arguments over the proper interpretation of God's infallible "truth," there can be no question as to the original intent of these laws - a recipe for disaster which even the most casual of Christians simply can't ignore.

Death to the gays? The atheists? Your family?

The choice is yours - either wholly *embrace* these deadly ideologies as the authoritative Word of God, and be found guilty by association - OR - *reject* it, all, entirely. I did. Sure, I may have lost a few Christian friends along the way, but I'll no longer leave a legacy of shame on this issue when I'm gone.

www.AwkwardMomentsBible.com/RecipeForDisaster

Happy New Year, Baby J!

Ugh... enough with foreskin already, right? As always, don't blame me - the Bible is full of this creepy stuff! Heck, several churches are eager to show off the *real* foreskin of Jesus in glass museum cases.

One of the odd things about this verse is how the circumcision of Christ is often quoted as "proof" of the divinity of Jesus, through the fulfillment of prophecy. Oh, really? In case you haven't been paying attention - no, Jesus wasn't circumcised for medical reasons or to fulfill prophecy, His tiny little penis was cut on the eighth day, just like every other unlucky baby Jewish boy! Why? So God could tell Jews from gentiles, it was the Law! "Lift your robes and show me your covenant keeper, kids!" Ugh. Paul even circumcised Timothy before suggesting his own changes to God's heavenly mutilation mandate.

I just wonder which lucky mohel got to perform the *metzitzah b'peh* on the little Lord Jesus. (The Bible makes no distinction regarding the orthodoxy of Mary and Joseph's faith, so we'll never know...)

www.AwkwardMomentsBible.com/MoreForeskin

Speak Softly, Carry A Big... Sword!

Lucky for us, modern Christianity has largely fallen away from the Biblical roots that were called upon as justification for the brutality of The Crusades. As more prosperity-preaching megachurches appear in yuppie neighborhoods while the virus of Ghandi-wannabe church plants pop-up in strip malls, it isn't too difficult to understand why the "average" Christian seems to have such little knowledge of who this Jesus guy really was. To most Christians He is the Meek and Mild, Wonderful Counselor, Everlasting Father, the Prince of... Peace?

For some it's merely honest-but-lazy ignorance, having never actually opened the Good Book that is the basis for their bumper stickers and weekly social clubs. Others though, after catching an enlightening glimpse behind the curtain that is scripture, secretly don't want to dig any deeper on their own, instead merely follow their pastor's lead as they learn/yearn to avoid the awkward stuff together.

According to the Bible, Jesus was not only the Son of God, but God, Himself. (Sort of. Somehow He was also an invisible spirit with really low self esteem. More on this later...) Once the constantly wrathful, vengeful God was able to find His way into the flesh, it should really come as no surprise that Jesus often displayed many of the less-than-desirable personality traits found in His own Father/Self's earlier appearances in the Old Testament. These sorts of cameos are often ignored or dismissed by average Christians as mysterious metaphor or antiquated allegory.

> *"Do not think I have come to bring peace on earth. I do not bring peace, but a sword!"*
> - Jesus

Many armchair Christian apologists have been trained to refute these words of Jesus by arguing, "He didn't mean a real sword - it's a metaphor for the Word of God!" Uh...

1. Says who? Did Jesus really know that, decades or centuries later, complete strangers would be outlining His life in a series of gospels, always looking for ways to add metaphorical poetry and prose to His biography?

2. What about the troubling, "I do not bring peace," part of this passage? After all, isn't "Prince of Peace" literally one of His most popular nicknames, based on the fulfillment of prophecy of the coming Messiah according to a nudist prophet (Isaiah 9:6)?

Was Jesus a flame-loving aichmomaniac or not? Was Jesus the Prince of Peace or wasn't He?

For answers, I think it's fair to examine what Jesus is reported to have actually said about Himself. After all, who would you be more inclined to believe if you met him on the street today? Jesus, speaking for Himself, or - an apologetic pastor with a livelihood to defend by perfecting explanations of "what Jesus really meant" and how Christ's very own disciples somehow understood their own leader less than modern pastors, thousands of years later? If the latter is your preference, I can assure you that there are plenty of "metaphorical experts" to be found at local churches and endless blogs of armchair apologists. Though, if the growing thousands of divergent denominations are any indication, beware - they'll probably never agree on the finer points of, *"What Jesus Really Meant."*

www.AwkwardMomentsBible.com/SwordOfChrist

Jesus, Relationship Expert

In Philip Yancey's book *Reaching for the Invisible God* (Zondervan, 2000), he tells readers, "getting to know God is a lot like getting to know a person. You spend time together, whether happy or sad. You laugh together. You weep together. You fight and argue, then reconcile." This once resonated with me so deeply that I gifted the book to many friends.

I'm sure you've heard the popular Christian mantra, "It's not about religion - it's about relationship!" It wasn't until I began to honestly struggle with the ambiguity of faith that I had a life-changing epiphany. It seems that the only people who *truly* believe in this "relationship" are the troubled minds you see on the evening news trying to convince a jury of their peers that it was God who told them to... [you fill in the blank].

All of the interactions to which Yancey refers require the active participation and involvement of two individuals in a functional relationship. Anything else is just, dare I say, 'make believe' - once a cute game for children, but when played by adults there are other words for it - dysfunctional at best, delusional at worst. I fully understand that many devout Christians would be deeply offended by having their "personal relationship with Christ" be challenged under such derogatory terms. But, I must ask... if this personal relationship is not make believe - please explain how one might verify the difference between an *authentic* claim of a "healthy" divine relationship and that of a dangerous *imaginary* one?

You laugh together? You weep together? The very notion that the same things would make you and the creator of the universe happy or sad goes back to the very first illustration in this book. Yet, many base their entire faith around such notions of grandiose self importance. *Your* emotions, *your* needs placated by *your* god(s) in *your* image.

Even Yancey's title spoils the surprise and does no favors to Christianity by openly admitting to worship an ***Invisible God***, a celestial "My Buddy" doll that will never talk back. Unlike a real-life relationship, a 'personal relationship' with such an invisible, silent, and absentee God of your own choosing requires no communication or compromises. No risks, just rewards. How convenient... and dysfunctional.

www.AwkwardMomentsBible.com/Relationship

*Un*Conditional Love

Christians often complain about outsiders "cherry picking" random verses from the Bible, taking them out of context in an effort to give their faith a black eye. I don't disagree - it happens all the time and drives me crazy! In fact, it happens almost as often as the inverse, when pastors do the exact same thing with strategically opposite motives in mind. Let's take the well known John 15:13, for example:

"There is no greater love than for someone to lay down their life for a friend." - Jesus

How many Christians have heard the first half of this emotional edict preached from the pulpit? Beautiful selflessness, isn't it? It likely conjures up feelings you have for one of your closest friends - such selfless and unconditional love. But, how often does the pastor continue on with the very next verse, John 15:14, straight from the mouth of Jesus?

"You can only be my friends if you do whatever I tell you to do." - Jesus

Hmm... Suddenly this friendship feels a little one-sided, doesn't it? You are likely no longer thinking of your best friend but maybe back to a childhood bully who would order other kids around the playground. This leaves one to wonder about their own relationship with Jesus. In order to be His "friend," do I *also* have to do whatever He tells me; steal a donkey, lie to authorities, act blind so He can heal me, leave my family, and eat His flesh? If you ever challenged a bully on the playground, you likely know the answer - there's only room for *one* dictatorial megalomaniac in any relationship. If His words above are to be believed, as Jesus says:

"Anyone who is not with me is against me..."

Talk about a cheap ultimatum. It appears Christianity might not actually be about the unconditional love from, and relationship with, the savior of the universe (as we've been led to believe). Context, indeed. Don't even get me started on John 3:16. (Oh, wait - it's next!)

www.AwkwardMomentsBible.com/Conditional

In Summary

You've seen it referenced on highway billboards and painted on the faces of sports fans on TV. If you asked most (Biblically literate) Christians to choose the most powerful verse of the Bible, they wouldn't hesitate to name John 3:16. But why? Even in ministry I never disagreed over the power of John 3:16, but for completely opposite reasons. In short, I thought it was a horrible evangelism tool! Capricious in character and sinister in motive, no other verse makes such fantastic claims, threats, and promises that nobody could ever prove.

But, what do *you* think? Using the space below, deconstruct and expand each turn of phrase using your Biblical knowledge in order to gain a little personal perspective on this verse. A few caveats of context - remember that: 1) God once flooded the entire world, 2) This whole concept of "perishing" (hell) didn't exist until Jesus came onto the scene, and, 3) How many witnesses have come forward to testify about eternal life?

For God so loved the world

that He gave His one and only Son,

that whoever believes in Him

shall not perish

but have eternal life.

Use the link below to print the form and upload a picture of your translation. Be sure to check out other people's perspectives on this (in)famous verse:

www.AwkwardMomentsBible.com/John316

The *One* Unforgiveable Sin

For decades now, I've been close friends with an amazingly talented and influential human rights activist (and agnostic pacifist) who regularly puts his own life in danger in the far reaches of the world in order to fight for the most basic human rights of absolute strangers. He's always been one of my favorite people on the planet, a truly selfless servant of humanity, constantly putting the "greater good" ahead of his own needs, an inspiration to all who know him, regardless of one's beliefs.

Sadly, he's destined to burn in hell for all eternity! Like many, he happened to grow up in a culture where horrifically unthinkable blasphemous phrases like, "God Damn It," "Holy Shit," and "Jesus Fucking Christ" were used as everyday language, mere colloquialisms of general exclamation to be muttered any time a toe was stubbed or a glass was dropped on the kitchen floor. As such, he's now doomed, never to be forgiven. *The mortal sin!*

Now, just try to imagine the Holy Spirit, an equal member of the triune God, the alleged co-founder of the entire universe - watching a lifelong foreign aid worker building a water filtration system for a remote tribe in eastern Tanzania when a pipe cutter malfunctions, cleaving the man's finger from his hand. The only course of action upon hearing a common obscenity leave the man lips is to send the servant of humanity to suffer in hell for all eternity? Well, fine - if that somehow helps you feel supernaturally superior to my buddy, the living saint, fine - believe whatever you want. I just pray that you never stumble barefoot onto a Lego™.

Meanwhile, there are still blasphemy laws on the books around the world today - designed to punish anyone who claims God can't defend Himself. You know, by... creating specific laws *to* defend God *because* He *can't* defend Himself. Oh, the irony!

In honor of this scripture, I'd like to share my late grandmother's favorite cocktail hour bit:

"I just wish you wouldn't deny the Holy Spirit, dear - it's blasphemy!"
"Aw, don't worry, momma. When I die, the Holy Spirit and I - we'll be closer than ever!"
"Oh, that's wonderful to hear, honey.- thank you."
"Yeah, because then I won't exist either!"

www.AwkwardMomentsBible.com/MortalSin

Monotheism - Made To Order!

"These three are one..." The Latin Vulgate finally made it official in the 4th century - Christianity was a monotheistic marvel of the *One* Almighty God.

That is, until Desiderius Erasmus almost screwed it all up in 1516 when he released the first Bible based solely on the earliest Greek texts. The problem was - he wasn't able to find the crucial trinitarian phrase, "these three are one" in *any* of the original Greek. The short-but-crucial "Johannine Comma" simply did *not* exist in the ancient pre-Vulgate sources!

A scandal then erupted as authorities tried to have Erasmus' translation banned, accusing him of heresy for undermining the doctrine of the Trinity, a *deadly* serious offense at the time. Then, as if by magic, Erasmus was supplied with a portion of an unknown Greek manuscript (most likely forged) and he dutifully agreed to update the next edition of his translation (likely to avoid death). A century later this new work would be the basis for the King James Bible still used today. Monotheism - *made to order.*

www.AwkwardMomentsBible.com/MonoMath

Take Your Medicine!

When a family member heard that I was taking my first mission trip to Africa years ago, they sent a very earnest letter of concern that ended, "I'll be praying that you'll be able to rid them of their primitive witchcraft."

Uh… if you want witchcraft, look no further than the Bible. And, I'm not talking about the talking animals and burning bushes of the time of Moses, I'm talking about the beliefs and instructions of Jesus himself.

Why exactly are we no longer practicing this laughably gruesome miracle cure for leprosy today? I'd suggest that, from tsunamis to psoriasis, society has (largely) outgrown the superstitious ancestral ignorance that has long threatened progress for fear

of change. Or, what do I know - I'm not a chemist. Maybe Rifampicin is still made from dead birds, sheep, yarn, and a touch of oil and flour?

On the other hand, why do you think most Christians have never heard of these fantastical passages on Sunday morning? After all, leprosy was considered a sin, right? And, the church is all about freeing us from our sins, right? Could it be because previous focus group testing showed that preaching about "primitive witchcraft" from the pulpit might reflect poorly in… the offering dish? Nah…
SIDE NOTE: I would have paid GOOD money to see the this scene reenacted at one of Billy Graham's "crusades." Can you imagine?

www.AwkwardMomentsBible.com/VoodooJesus

Opportunistic Opthamologist

Lordy! If you think a little spit in the ocular cavity is awkward, you should have seen Christ's cure for prostate cancer! Whenever people ask me why Jesus was finally arrested, I tell them to try this little stunt on a stranger in front of a crowd at the county fair and let me know how things work out.

I've always found it *interesting* that no recipients of Christ's amazing miracles were moved enough by their life-changing experiences to become full-fledged disciples or go on to write first-person gospels of their own. How ungrateful! I mean, sure - they would have most likely been illiterate nomads, but it's almost as if, without any evidence to prove otherwise, these miraculous narratives could be interpreted as nothing more than entertaining bedtime stories full of interesting characters with made-to-order defects that were just waiting to be healed by a wise and powerful magician! You know - someone like David Blaine.

Indeed, it was precisely these sorts of alleged stunts that led religious leaders to suspect… fraud. When asked to replicate such miraculous feats on demand, Jesus basically said, "Eh, maybe later - the light's not right." You'd think one of His success stories would have come forward to testify on His behalf, but they mysteriously all went missing from the historic record, disappearing unnoticed into anonymous ambiguity.

Some might say, the stuff of legends. That reminds me, I wonder what happened to Lazarus?

www.AwkwardMomentsBible.com/JesusSpit

Dog Lady & Demon Child

If you ever want to waste a few minutes investigating the gymnastic capabilities of the modern Christian apologist's brain, be sure to do a few web searches about this passage to learn:

1. Even though Jesus referred to the woman as a dog and refused to help her until she submissively conceded that she was a dog, well… that's not what He *really* meant. After all, He did eventually help her, right? Sure, right after He insulted her (and anybody not of Jewish ancestry).

2. Even though Jesus repeatedly tells others that He came to save *only* those of Jewish descent living *at the time*, he really died on cross so that modern white middle-class Americans could have their wishes granted. After all, He died for them!

3. Pay no attention to the demon-infested little girl levitating in the corner. Because, well, you know - that sort of thing just coincidentally stopped occurring once audio and video recording capabilities could be carried in your pocket. Sure, we now have copious video evidence of rare animal behavior, random car accidents, and police violence, but - not a single video of demon possession - even with over 500,000 reported exorcisms per year - among Catholics alone? Hmm… Of course, demon possession is still a real thing - as long you have enough faith to believe in it! Nothing sells faith like the fear of the boogeyman. Just ask Frank Peretti.

But, indeed - it was a miracle that Jesus helped the woman at all, since, as we learned by reading the real Ten Commandments, the role of a Jew was to NEVER make treaties with outsiders. Oh, that Jesus - He's a very naughty boy.

www.AwkwardMomentsBible.com/DogLady

Live By Faith, *Die* By Faith

"We don't have a flu season. We've already had our shot. Jesus himself gave us the flu shot. He redeemed us from the curse of flu and we receive it, and we take it, and we are healed by his stripes!"

These are not the words of a "fringe" fundamentalist holed up in the woods somewhere, but current medical advice given by Gloria Copeland, an influential member of President Trump's Evangelical Advisory Board. In a special video presentation released during the worst flu season in U.S. history which, at the time of airing, had already killed 53 children and hospitalized countless adults, the prominent televangelist told her sizable audience, "Just keep saying that 'I'll never have the flu, I'll never have the flu.' Inoculate yourself with the Word of God!" Now, if only I could find my ruby slippers!

This Biblical teaching is anything but "fringe" and is hardly limited to curing influenza. In fact, at the time of this writing, Paula White, official "spiritual adviser" to the President of the United States and chairwoman of his Evangelical Advisory Board has joined forces for a "Miracle Crusade" faith-healing tour with self-appointed "Apostle" David E. Taylor who claims to regularly cure cancer, spinal cord injuries, and, wait for it… raise people from the dead via text message.

All tax-free and protected from fraud litigation under the protections afforded by "religious freedoms" guaranteed by the U.S. Constitution. Again, just to be clear - these are not claims being made by "fringe" con artists lurking in the shadows, but by a megachurch pastor who gave an *official* invocation on the steps of the U.S. Capitol Building during the inauguration of the 45th President of the United States! Anything but "fringe."

Why does this matter?

Because children are dying, dammit!

I actually happen to believe that forcing medical treatments on lucid adults against their will is a very slippery slope. However, it's your right as an adult to make a conscious choice to forgo basic medical treatment available in hopes that Jesus will cure your diabetes - even if this decision eventually leads to your untimely death, leading your family to hide your rotting corpse in the attic for six months while they continue to pray for Jesus to bring you back from the dead. (As was the case of Peter Wold of Ontario, Canada.)

However, it's an entirely different matter to force those beliefs on children who depend on the sanity of others to keep them, fed, clothed, and, well… alive - only to have them suffer and die in a bizarre test of a parent's faith in the efficacy of prayer.

Take for example, 12 year-old Syble Rossiter who died as the result of ketoacidosis after her parents withheld "necessary and adequate" medical

attention for her Type 1 diabetes. What about 16 year-old Austin Sprout who died of a simple infection after his parents refused medical care? Or, infant David Hinkman who died of pneumonia after his parents denied access to doctors. After 9 year-old Aaron Grady died when his mother refused standard treatment for his diabetes, she testified, "I felt like God would heal him." How about the agony 17 year-old Zachery Swezey went through when he died after his appendix burst and, instead of taking a quick trip to the hospital, his parents called church elders to pray over him with anointing oils. Neal Beagley died when he was only 16 due to simple urinary tract infection that was only treated with prayer. Just a year earlier his older sister was charged with the death of her own daughter, 15 month-old Ava, who was denied antibiotics for a cyst on her neck that worsened to cause a blood infection and pneumonia - all while church leaders gathered to pray, anoint the baby with oil, and feed her wine. And don't even get me started on the Schaibles who managed to kill *two* of their children before being stopped by the courts.

Please Consider: These are only the cases that make headlines when an "outsider" complains to authorities and a child's unnecessary death makes the local news. Meanwhile, certain church cemeteries continue to fill up with children, largely unnoticed (ignored) by authorities and press.

I must ask - where is the outrage? Where are the protest marches? The vast majority of Christians vocally oppose abortion because of the "rights of the fetus" - yet when it comes to the rights of a living child, the church is largely silent. Why? Because by denying the power of prayer, they'd be thereby denying the power of faith, the legitimacy of scripture and the very existence of God.

Instead of vigorously denouncing these acts, moderate Christians are quick to hide behind theological semantics to label these parents as "fringe believers" or "not true Christians" – all while attempting to distance their own eerily similar beliefs about faith and prayer as far from these parents as possible.

But, again, we aren't talking about fringe fanatics here - faith healing "crusades" are big business. A travel package to Paula White's next "Miracle Crusade" will run you $2,166, though, admittedly, that is a fraction of an actual spinal cord surgery. Of course, there will be no refunds - if you aren't healed, it's your own fault for not believing enough!

I am happy to see that more states have begun to crack down on this insanity in recent years as a few parents are finally being convicted charges like "manslaughter" or "neglect" for refusing basic

life-saving medicine in deference to prayer. However, "manslaughter" doesn't adequately describe these deaths, implying a tragic accident that was somehow out of one's control - much in the same way "neglect" equates these crimes with a sad visual of a struggling single parent who just can't afford to keep their children fed and clothed. No, these deaths were no accident, but carefully planned and executed: "*If* our child gets sick, *then* we will *withhold* treatment." That's no accident, it is negligent homicide – all taught by their church, using the Bible as an instruction manual - largely protected today by "religious freedom exemptions" amended to the Constitution and state laws.

Serious Question: While more parents may soon find themselves being prosecuted to the fullest extent of available laws, no longer protected by specific religious freedom exemptions, why is there no responsibility on behalf of the churches that indoctrinate parents into actions that specifically lead to these completely avoidable deaths? In many cases, clergy take an active role in the prayer and anointing sessions while encouraging (daring) the parents to rely on the the power of prayer while their child's brain boils from an easily treatable fever. To me, these clergy should not only be charged as an "accessory" to murder but as a "conspirator" for organizing the scheme to begin with. It's simple - if a pharmaceutical company is found to be deliberately distributing false treatments, they are prosecuted. Why aren't churches being charged for similar crimes?

It's almost as if churches are above the law? Oh, wait – that's right, it is the poor Christians who are so horribly persecuted in this country. You know, aside from literally getting away with murder.

www.AwkwardMomentsBible.com/FaithKillers

The Chosen Ones

So… first God created the Garden of Eden to feed and shelter His people. Then an ark was built to save his creation from Himself. Later, He set aside a special land just for the Jews. Eventually, according to the New Testament, this same "God of the Prophets" - Noah, Abraham, Moses, Isaiah, and Ezekiel created a brand new special place, indeed - just for His 'chosen ones.' Hell.

Isn't it interesting how Christians are so quick to speak of the horrors of the Holocaust, but are just as quick to ignore how their own beliefs include a 180° plot twist where their God suddenly decides to sentence *every* Jew, His own "chosen ones," to an eternal life of... horrific torture? My mind has never been able to get around the fact that most modern evangelicals support Israel in life while condemning the Jews in death. Of course, not for their actions and behaviors, but for merely *not* believing in theirs, the latest of a long line of false prophets - an ancient apocalyptic preacher who claimed to be God Himself, reborn in the flesh. The exact sort of false prophet God himself spent most of the Old Testament warning His chosen ones not to trust:

*"There will **never** be one after me.*
I am the Lord, and apart from me
there is no savior" - Isaiah 43:10-11

*"I, your Lord will **never** change."*
- Malachai 3:6

"I am the first and I am the last;
*apart from me **there is no other God.**"*
- Isaiah 44:6

You can't blame the Jews for following God's own strict warnings against worshiping false prophets. If God, in His infinite wisdom really wanted the Jews to drop everything and follow His Son/Self, maybe He shouldn't have been so adamant about being the ONLY true god to begin with!

Consider - these are the very Jews He spent so much time, energy, and effort protecting in the Old Testament, creating covenants, setting aside land, squashing any enemies in their path. Then what? God, arms folded, smiling over Auschwitz as the Jesus-denying Jews are gassed and burned, knowing that He'd eventually meet the Jews who managed to escape the Nazis during their final "Judgment" and finish the job himself? If you are offended by the idea of God smiling down as His people are tortured in life, let me remind you that it was He who later invented their torture in death - with not one mention of hell until Jesus came on the scene.

So, then - more genius work there - setting His chosen ones up for an eternally fatal bait-and-switch of His own failed design. Praise be to His illogical name. Maybe if He were half as omnipotent as He appears to be incompetent He would have had a little foresight into the errors of His plan. Likewise, with His popularity being so clearly important to His god-sized ego, maybe He'd make it a little more

obvious to the modern, thinking, scientifically literate world that He exists at all. But, no - an eternal hell for His most devout, that makes sense, right? What's worse - a German nutcase killing the Jews, or God 2.0 changing all the rules to torture them for all eternity?

Conversely, while all the Jews are suffering their eternal torment, as Sarah Silverman so astutely points out in her HBO special *We Are Miracles*, "You can be Hitler and go to confession and say 'forgive me father, I killed six million Jews...' and Hitler goes to heaven. **Hitler goes to heaven!**" Yet, God's torture of the Jews will *never* end. Ugh.

www.AwkwardMomentsBible.com/ChosenOnes

I'm Guessing That's A 'No' On Dessert?

Is this really how a Prince of Peace would talk to His disciples? No, this is how a militaristic cult leader would speak to his army of brain-washed minions. Now, imagine if the creator of the universe came with a message of profound unity instead of this promise of destroying otherwise perfectly happy families. Bah!

I won't bore you with the details of my own family struggles in recent years after merely hinting that I might be questioning my faith, the validity of the Bible, the church, or even God Himself. Let's just say that voices have been raised (not mine), glasses have been spilled (again, not mine), and family members have been asked to leave one another's home (and I didn't even get dessert). The thing is, I know I'm not alone in enjoying the manifestations of Christ's awesome divisiveness, so I'd welcome you to read others' stories (or share your own) here:

www.AwkwardMomentsBible.com/Division

Not Now, Momma!

So... He can't be bothered by His own family members (who are literally trying to save His life),

but He wants a personal relationship with you? Sounds like a really great guy... What's that rule about only dating men who are good to their mothers? Brides of Christ - if this is your idea of an eternal savior, you might want to get a pre-nup.

www.AwkwardMomentsBible.com/MommyIssues

Snakes, Poisons, and Demons, Too!

Yet another preacher was recently bitten by a poisonous snake while giving a sermon at his church. He didn't die. Though, his father did years earlier, as did his father's father before that - just like many of the snake handlers who have died performing similar stunts for their traveling circus.

The thing is - most modern Bibles agree, if only hidden in the footnotes, that this whole notion of death-defying snake handling and poison-drinking is made-up nonsense, the last twelve verses of Mark's gospel being added centuries later (Indeed, verses 16:9–20 are not even present in two 4th-century manuscripts that contain the earliest complete manuscripts of Mark - Codex Sinaiticus and Codex Vaticanus). However, it's not just snake handling that was inserted into the series of verses. What is known as the Great Commission, the missional edict to go forth into the world and evangelize to others was added here are well.

In fact, the last three words of Mark's original gospel were simply, *"They were afraid."*

Who added the final action-packed 12 verses remains a bit of a mystery. Yet, it begs the question - what else has been added to God's Word by the very men who would later benefit from such alterations? What stops others from altering the interpretations of the Bible to fit their own cultural, political, or personal agendas? Well, not much - just ask Erasmus! Or, take a quick look at the "new and improved " translations of ancient texts that grace the shelves of Christian bookstores everywhere. Some are even adorned with fuzzy pink fur and bedazzled with sparkly jewels. Because, well, you know - Christianity is about holiness and reverence.

The reason we didn't illustrate this passage is because, unlike the church, we'd rather not assist in perpetuating fraudulent scripture. Heathens have standards, you know.

www.AwkwardMomentsBible.com/Mark16

Fools For Christ

Among the most popular mantras passed around within Christian culture, this particular rallying cry has proven to be one of the trickiest to tackle. In fact, just choosing how to illustrate this concept proved to be problematic. Do we illustrate the boy to encompass a sort of prideful willing ignorance that seems to be directly in line with the *"Fool For Christ"* bumper stickers, memes, and t-shirts? Or, do we try to show the sad underlying reality as the pursuit of discovery, knowledge, and wisdom are squashed from another generation in order to make room for... Jesus?

As an "outsider" there's really no good way to address the issue of anti-intellectualism that is becoming increasingly pervasive among certain subgroups of Christian culture today. It's a "momma's cooking" sort of thing - while many believers proudly preach, write, sing, brag and high-five each other for being "fools for Christ" amid growing resentment for the "liberal elite" and academic institutions - the moment a secular person expresses concerns over this destructive tenet of their faith, cries of persecution and allegations of attacks on their religious freedom ring out. Sigh...

But, back to the verses at hand, I guess the big question is simply, why? Why would a god need to use trickery to obfuscate wisdom from the masses? Or, worse yet - why would any god require the wholehearted acceptance of "foolishness" from His followers as a sign of faith and devotion? Is that really how an omnipotent god would want to choose his "team" for the big game? Even in my days of ministry, this notion of willful foolishness from the Apostle Paul rubbed me the wrong way and seemed quite counterproductive to the case for Christianity's long-term survival. *[Cognitive dissonance event: #1,837]*

Today, as I read these passages from Paul, the forefather of the Christian church, I don't think backward to grown men high-fiving each other at a church camping retreat, I think forward - of what is being taught to their children in churches around the world today.

If you hear something often enough, you'll start to believe it. Believe it long enough, you'll start to act like it – a self-fulfilling prophecy. There should be no pride in willful ignorance and no child should be conditioned to proudly play the fool - not to please their parents, or gods. (Ultimately, it was this realization that helped choose the boy's trapped emotion for the illustration for the book.)

What exactly must a Christian do in order to prove an adequate level of foolishness to God? Walk down the street wearing a provocative shirt, or not wear any clothes at all like Isaiah? Or is it enough to, as the Apostle Paul put it, simply *believe* the *"foolishness"* of scripture?

On the other hand, it should be pointed out that Paul's teachings again appear to conflict with Christ:

"Whosoever shall call another a fool shall be in danger of hell fire." – Jesus (Matthew 5:22)

It should also be noted that Jesus called many people "fools," including His own disciples and pretty much anyone who didn't agree with Him. (Matthew 23:17, Luke 11:40, Luke 24:25.)

www.AwkwardMomentsBible.com/ProudFools

Actions, Not Beliefs

"Jesus, it's like they're begging to get punched in the face," a colleague gasped as we watched a few members of Westboro Baptist Church converging on a private funeral, each holding a brightly colored sign stating simply, "God Hates Fags."

"Yeah," I replied sarcastically. "I can't imagine why anybody would hate us."

I'm not sure if it was because I said it out loud, but this was the first time it really dawned on me - US. Whether we liked it or not, no matter how much we tried to be the "good guys" for Jesus, the fact of the matter was, we were part of the same club, guilt by association. Sure, it's always easy to dismiss and distance your own faith from the bizarre marketing tactics of loudmouths with bullhorns, but one thing is now very clear - Christianity is only as strong as its weakest, most despicable teachings and teachers, of which there is a ready supply.

Before I go on, I think it is necessary to make an important distinction; while Christians often confess to detest atheists primarily because of their **beliefs**, it is more often the **actions** of their fellow Christians that atheists take vocal issue with.

Even today, as I write, there are several pieces of legislation being debated across the United States that claim to "protect religious freedoms" like child marriages, workplace discrimination, faith healing exemptions, and religious indoctrination in public schools. Just as God never complains or objects, He also never condones or applauds, leading one to conclude - Christians are not "hated" because of their love for Christ, but for the many abhorrent behaviors in which they partake in His name.

On the other hand, one must also recognize what appears to be part of a deliberate strategy - almost a craving to be hated, persecuted, or even martyred as an opportunity to show just how deeply their faith runs (in the face of opposition). Just this morning I came across two articles by *The Christian Post*, published one after another:

"Atheism Needs To Be Uprooted And Destroyed As An Enemy To Human Society."
[Uhh... because a scientist asked a rhetorical question regarding meat being "grown" in labs?]

"Facing Anti-Christian Hysteria - Bias And Bigotry Is Now A Reality In America."
[Oh, *now* it's a reality? *Now?* Welcome to the party, Dr. Amnesia - you're a little late!]

I'll just close by admitting that I went through a brief-but-dark period after leaving the church during which I no longer felt that God deserved my love and I began to recognize that many of the Bible's teachings (that I once perpetuated) deserved only condemnation. However, it wasn't long before this hatred turned into pity as I was able to take a step back and view Jesus as a man, through the eyes of the religious leaders of the day - a troubled young apocalpytic preacher who, according to His own family, had *"gone insane."* Soon, this pity turned back into love for Christ, but a new sort of love. A purer love than Christianity could ever compel of its own followers - a love that comes without risk of threat or promise of reward. The same kind of love I've come to have for the many Christians who know not what they do as they act out against their neighbor - not of their own volition, but the result of generations of cultural evolution - normalized through accepted idnoctrination.

"They will hate you because of me," Jesus said - another one of Christ's prophecies that I now reject - offering instead nothing but understanding, pity, and love for those who bring division in His name. Be careful of the company you keep, friends - you might one day be found guilty.

www.AwkwardMomentsBible.com/HateJesus

No True Christian

What common arguments reveal about faith culture.

NOTHING WITHOUT JESUS!

OUT OF CONTEXT!

CHRISTIAN NATION

I'M NOT AN APE

From the inbox of
HORUS GILGAMESH

working cover

Hate mail, fan mail, and a few
thoughts on faith and culture taken from
everday conversations with strangers

October 2018

NoTrueChristian.com

Made in United States
North Haven, CT
03 April 2023

34963579R00053